RECIPES MY
MOTHER
TAUGHT ME

To Laurie,
My science buddy!
Thanks for all the
support!

Don't forget to
add the love!
— Judi Ü Guisado

Jeanette Holsten

RECIPES MY
MOTHER
TAUGHT ME

Jeanette Acuna Holsten
and
Judi Holsten Guizado

Northwest Publishing Inc.
Salt Lake City, Utah

Recipes My Mother Taught Me

For information address: Northwest Publishing, Inc.
6906 South 300 West, Salt Lake City, Utah 84047

SCM 06 16 94

PRINTING HISTORY
First Printing 1994

ISBN: 1-56901-130-3

NPI books are published by Northwest Publishing, Incorporated,
6906 South 300 West, Salt Lake City, Utah 84047.
The name "NPI" and the "NPI" logo are trademarks belonging to
Northwest Publishing, Incorporated.

PRINTED IN THE UNITED STATES OF AMERICA.
10 9 8 7 6 5 4 3 2 1

This book is dedicated with love to our mothers,
and their mothers, and their mothers…

TABLE OF CONTENTS

MEXICAN FAMILY MATRIARCH
LUCY ACUNA

MAIN DISHES:

DOWN-HOME FAMILY MATRIARCH OPAL HOLSTEN

MAIN DISHES:

SIDE DISHES:

DESSERTS:

ITALIAN FAMILY MATRIARCHS
ANNA SEPE AND CONNIE SEPE ACUNA

MAIN DISHES:

SIDE DISHES:

DESSERTS:

FOREWORD

This book contains traditional recipes which have been handed down in our family for generations; from mother to daughter; from mother-in-law to daughter-in-law; from grandmother to granddaughter. Until this time, they have not been recorded in written form, but kept alive in the minds and hearts of the matriarchs who have raised and nurtured each subsequent generation.

We hope that you will enjoy these treasures. It is with a deep sense of family pride and love that they are offered.

Jeanette Acuna Holsten
Judi Holsten Guizado

OUR "MOM" FAMILY TREE OF FOUR GENERATIONS

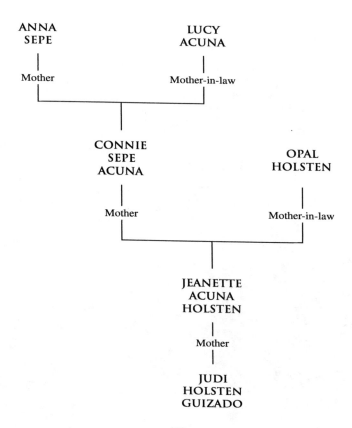

ANNA
SEPE

|
Mother

LUCY
ACUNA

|
Mother-in-law

CONNIE
SEPE
ACUNA

|
Mother

OPAL
HOLSTEN

|
Mother-in-law

JEANETTE
ACUNA
HOLSTEN

|
Mother

JUDI
HOLSTEN
GUIZADO

MEXICAN DISHES

MEXICAN FAMILY MATRIARCH
LUCY ACUNA

CHICKEN AND BREAD

Beside traditional Mexican dishes, Grandma Lucy was famous for making unique meals from unusual combinations of simple ingredients. What resulted was some incredible food.

—J.H.

8 pieces of chicken (wings, legs, thighs, or any combination)
⅓ cup flour
1 teaspoon salt
⅛ teaspoon pepper
4 tablespoons vegetable oil
1 cup onion, finely chopped
1 (16 ounce) can whole peeled tomatoes
3 cups water
2 tablespoons chopped mild green chiles
1 one pound loaf French bread, unsliced

1. In a small bowl, mix together flour, salt, and pepper.
2. Dip chicken in flour mixture to coat.
3. In a skillet, heat oil over medium flame.
4. Brown chicken in oil until both sides are golden brown. (NOTE: Chicken will not be cooked through at this point.)
5. Remove chicken and reserve drippings. Drain chicken on paper toweling to remove oil.
6. Sauté onions in chicken drippings until soft. Remove from heat.

7. In a separate bowl, break tomatoes into smaller pieces.
8. In a large kettle or pot, place onions and drippings. Add tomatoes, water, green chiles, and chicken pieces.
9. Cover and bring to a boil. Reduce heat and simmer for 45 minutes. Then turn off heat.
10. Break bread into chunks, approximately 2 inches square.
11. Gently stir bread into chicken mixture, allowing bread to soak up juices. Serve immediately.

Makes 4–5 servings.

CHILI BEANS

2 cups dry pink beans
5 cups water
8 cups water
1 ½ pounds hamburger
8 ounce can tomato sauce
1 cup water
2 teaspoons chili powder
2 teaspoons salt
⅛ teaspoon pepper
2 tablespoons dry onion
1 teaspoon cumin

1. Wash beans, removing any stones or debris. Drain.
2. Place beans in a large pot and cover with 5 cups of water. Let soak for 1 hour.
3. Drain and rinse beans. Return them to the pot and add 8 cups water.
4. Cover and bring to a boil. Reduce heat and simmer for 2 hours or until beans are tender.
5. In a skillet, brown hamburger. Drain off excess grease.
6. Add tomato sauce, 1 cup water, chili powder, salt, pep-

per, dry onion and cumin to the cooked hamburger.
7. Simmer hamburger mixture for 10 minutes.
8. Add hamburger mixture to beans in pot. Cover and simmer 1 hour.

Makes 5 servings.

CHORIZO AND POTATOES

Grandma Lucy prepared three hearty meals every Monday through Saturday to feed her family. They were hardworking people, employed in the construction and citrus industries. This was often served as a breakfast meal, along with fried eggs, refried beans, and tortillas.

—J.H.

5 medium potatoes, peeled
3 tablespoons oil
1 teaspoon salt
8 ounces beef or pork chorizo links (Mexican-style sausage)

1. Slice potatoes into 1/4 inch slices.
2. Heat oil in a heavy skillet.
3. Add potatoes to hot oil. Cover.
4. Stir frequently until the potatoes are lightly brown and almost cooked through.
5. Remove plastic casing from the chorizo links and lay on top of the browning potatoes.
6. Cover and cook five minutes until chorizo links start to soften.
7. Using a fork, break up chorizo and stir into the potatoes.
8. Cover and reduce heat, simmering for 30 minutes to allow flavors to blend and potatoes to become tender.

Makes 6 servings.

PINK BEANS AND HAM

3 cups dried pink beans
water for soaking
2-2 ½ pounds ham hock
8 cups water

1. Clean beans by spreading out a small amount and removing any stones or damaged beans. Rinse in a colander.
2. Place cleaned beans in a large pot. Cover with water and soak for 2 to 3 hours (or overnight, if possible).
3. Drain off soaking water. Add ham hock and 8 cups of water.
4. Cover and bring to a boil. Reduce heat to simmer. Cook for 4 to 5 hours, stirring occasionally. Should water start to evaporate to below the level of the beans, add a little more.

Makes about 6 cups.

To Make Fried Beans From Cooked Pink Beans:

1 teaspoon vegetable oil
2 cups beans, drained (reserve juice)
¼ cup reserved juice
¼ cup grated cheddar cheese

1. Heat oil in a heavy skillet over a medium-high flame.
2. Quickly fry beans in hot oil, stirring constantly.
3. Stir in juice.
4. Mash beans and juice with a potato masher.
5. Continue cooking 5 minutes over medium flame, stirring frequently.

6. Stir in cheese and remove from heat. Let stand 5 minutes to allow cheese to melt.

Makes 4 servings.

SHORT-CUT REFRIED BEANS

Over the years, the increasing demands on our time have resulted in some alterations of the classic dishes. This was Mom's way to make a very good imitation Grandma Lucy's beans without spending all day in the kitchen.

—J.H.

1 (30 ounce) can small red beans
2 tablespoons bacon fat
⅓ cup grated cheddar cheese

1. Melt bacon fat in a skillet over a low flame.
2. Drain off most of the liquid from the beans.
3. Add beans and reserved liquid to melted bacon fat.
4. Increase heat to medium flame and bring to a gentle boil.
5. Cook for 5 minutes, stirring occasionally.
6. With a potato masher or large fork, mash beans in the pan.
7. Cook for 2–3 minutes more to thicken, stirring constantly.
8. Stir in cheese. Remove from heat and let stand 5 minutes to let cheese melt.

Makes 4 servings.

MEXICAN STEW

2 pounds chuck steak
2 tablespoons vegetable oil
¼ teaspoon garlic powder
8 medium potatoes
1 cup sliced onion
2 cups water
1 ½ teaspoons salt
⅛ teaspoon pepper

1. Trim fat and bone from the meat. Cut meat into 1-inch cubes.
2. In a large pot or skillet, heat oil over a medium flame.
3. Add meat and garlic powder to hot oil. Sauté slowly, until pink color is gone from the meat.
4. Peel and cut potatoes into 1-inch cubes. Add to meat.
5. Cook meat and potatoes for 5–6 minutes, lightly browning meat and potatoes.
6. Stir in onion, water, salt, and pepper. Cover and bring to a boil.
7. Reduce flame and simmer for 1 ½ hours, or until meat and potatoes are tender.

Makes 6 servings.

NACHOS

2 ½ pounds 7-bone roast
1 (2 ½ ounce) package taco seasoning
2 cups water
2 cups masa harina (a fine corn flour)
1 cup warm water
¼ cup vegetable oil

1 ½ cups refried beans
¼ cup chopped green onions
½ cup sliced olives
2 cups grated cheddar cheese
Fresh tomato salsa #1 (See recipe on page 31.)

1. Cook meat with 2 cups water and taco seasoning in a pressure cooker for 35 minutes OR in a medium crock pot for 10 to 12 hours, until the meat shreds easily when pulled by a fork.
2. Remove meat and discard any bone or fat.
3. Shred meat into bite-sized pieces. Set aside.
4. In a bowl, mix together masa harina and warm water.
5. Shape dough into 12 equal-sized balls.
6. With a moistened hand, flatten each ball into a tortilla, about 5 inches in diameter.
7. Heat a heavy ungreased skillet or griddle over a high flame until very hot.
8. Cook each side of the tortilla about 45 seconds, or until tortilla is soft but cooked through.
9. Heat oil in a heavy skillet.
10. Quickly fry each side of tortilla until golden brown and crisp.
11. Drain tortilla on paper toweling to remove excess oil.
12. Place six fried tortillas in an ungreased 9 X 13-inch pan.
13. Spread half of the following ingredients over tortillas in this order: refried beans, meat, onion, olives, and cheese.
14. Repeat steps 12 and 13 for the second layer.
15. Place uncovered in an 350 degree oven for 5–10 minutes or until cheese is melted.
16. Spread salsa over the top OR serve on the side.

Makes 8 servings.

ENCHILADAS

I've been told this classic dish beckoned hungry family members home as the aroma of it baking wafted from Grandma Lucy's kitchen.

—J.G.

2 tablespoons oil
⅛ teaspoon garlic powder
¾ teaspoon ground cumin
1 tablespoon chili powder
½ teaspoon salt
2 cups water
4 ounces tomato sauce
2 tablespoons corn starch
¼ cup water
½ pound hamburger
¼ teaspoon salt
⅛ teaspoon pepper
⅛ teaspoon cumin
1 cup chopped black olives
4 cups shredded cheddar cheese
½ cup finely chopped onion
9 corn tortillas

1. In a skillet over medium flame, mix together oil, garlic powder, ¾ teaspoon ground cumin, chili powder, and ½ teaspoon salt.
2. Stir in cups 2 cups water and tomato sauce. Bring to a boil.
3. In a small bowl, mix together ¼ cup water and cornstarch until smooth.
4. While stirring the chili mixture, slowly add in the cornstarch mixture, stirring continuously. Bring to a rolling boil and cook until thickened.
5. In a separate skillet, brown hamburger. Drain off excess fat.
6. Stir in ¼ teaspoon salt, ⅛ teaspoon pepper, and ⅛ teaspoon cumin.

There are two different ways to prepare the enchiladas:

DIRECTIONS FOR ROLLED ENCHILADAS:

1. Spoon about ¼ cup of the chili sauce over the bottom of a 9 X 13-inch baking pan.
2. Dip a tortilla into the chili sauce to coat.
3. In the middle of the tortilla, spoon ½ tablespoon onion 1 tablespoon olives, ¼ cup cheese, and 1 heaping tablespoon hamburger.
4. Starting at one end, roll tortilla up into a tube, keeping all ingredients inside.
5. Place rolled enchilada in the prepared pan.
6. Repeat above steps for remaining tortillas.
7. Sprinkle any remaining cheese and olives on top of the rolled enchiladas.
8. Pour remaining sauce over enchiladas.
9. Cover with foil. Bake at 350 degrees for 1 hour and 15 minutes.

DIRECTIONS FOR LAYERED ENCHILADAS:

1. Spoon about 1/4 cup chili sauce over the bottom of an 8 X 8-inch baking pan.
2. Dip three tortillas into the chili sauce to coat and place flat on the bottom of the pan. (Tortillas will overlap.)
3. Spread a layer of 1 ½ tablespoons onion, 3 tablespoons olives, ¾ cups cheese, and 3 tablespoons meat over the tortillas.
4. Repeat for two more layers.
5. Sprinkle any remaining cheese and olives over the top layer.
6. Pour any remaining chili sauce over the enchiladas.
7. Cover with foil. Bake at 350 degrees for 1 hour and 15 minutes.

Makes 6 servings.

LAZY ENCHILADAS

Mom often made these for Dad when he had a craving for enchiladas, but she didn't have the time to roll or layer.

—*J.H.*

2 tablespoons vegetable oil
⅛ teaspoon garlic powder
¾ teaspoon ground cumin
2 teaspoons chili powder
½ teaspoon salt
2 cups water
½ cup tomato sauce
¼ cup chopped green onions
5 9-inch flour tortillas
½ cup sliced black olives
1 ½ cup grated cheddar OR jack cheese

1. In a large skillet, heat oil over a medium flame.
2. Stir in garlic powder, ground cumin, chili powder, and salt and heat through.
3. Stir in water and tomato sauce.
4. Bring to a boil.
5. Stir in onions and cook uncovered for 20 minutes, or until onions are soft.
6. Tear tortillas into small pieces, about 3 inches in diameter.
7. Stir in tortilla pieces, olives, and cheese.
8. Heat through until cheese starts to melt.
9. Remove skillet from the heat.
10. Let stand for 5 minutes to allow tortillas to absorb some of the liquid.

Makes 4 servings.

TACOS

1 medium potato, peeled and cut into 1-inch chunks
1 pound hamburger
⅛ teaspoon pepper
½ teaspoon salt
12 corn tortillas
oil for frying

Possible toppings:

grated cheddar and/or jack cheese
shredded lettuce
chopped tomato
sliced olives
mild taco sauce (recipe follows)

1. In a saucepan, boil potato chunks until just tender. Drain off excess water.
2. In a skillet, brown hamburger. Drain off excess fat.
3. Add salt and pepper to hamburger.
4. Mash potatoes (NOTE: DO NOT add anything except a little water if necessary to help in the mashing.)
5. Stir potatoes into hamburger. Set aside and keep warm.
6. Fry corn tortilla in the oil to form taco shells. Drain off excess oil.
7. Fill the taco shells with meat mixture, then add desired topping.

Makes 12 tacos.

MILD TACO SAUCE

1 (16 ounce) can whole tomatoes
⅓ cup coarsely chopped onions
¼ teaspoon salt
¼ teaspoon crushed red pepper

1. Put all ingredients into a blender.
2. Puree until smooth.
3. Refrigerate in a tightly sealed container for at least one hour.

Makes about 2 ½ cups.

———————

TWO-DAY TAMALES

In the Mexican tradition, tamales are often prepared for special occasions. Grandma Lucy proudly served these to family and friends every Christmas Eve.

—J.H.

½ pound dried corn husks (available in the produce department or in a Mexican specialty market)
1 (4 or 5 pound) pork roast
7 cups water
5 tablespoons chili powder
1 tablespoon + 1 teaspoon cumin
1 teaspoon garlic powder
2 ½ teaspoons salt
6 cups masa harina (a fine corn flour found in the baking section or in a Mexican specialty market)
2 cups lard OR vegetable shortening
4 ½ cups warm water
1 teaspoon salt

⅓ cup cornstarch
⅓ cup cold water
thin twine

DAY ONE:

1. Discard any damaged or dirty husks.
2. Place remaining husks in a large pot. Cover with water and allow to soak overnight to soften.
3. Trim any excess fat from the meat. Place in a large pot.
4. Add 7 cups of water, 4 tablespoons chili powder, 1 tablespoon cumin, and garlic powder.
5. Cover and bring to a boil.
6. Reduce heat and simmer for 3 ½ hours, or until meat is very tender.
7. Remove meat from pot, reserving all the juice. (NOTE: The juice will be used in several different steps in the preparation of tamales. Cover and store in refrigerator.)
8. Allow meat to cool until it is easy to handle.
9. Remove any fat or bone. Shred meat into small pieces.
10. Return 1 ⅔ cups of reserved juice to meat. Stir in 1 tablespoon chili powder, 1 teaspoon cumin, and salt to taste.
11. Refrigerate in covered bowl overnight.

DAY TWO:

1. Warm meat and reserved juice to room temperature.
2. In a large bowl, mix together masa harina, lard OR shortening, water, and salt.
3. Add 1 cup reserved meat juice, mixing together well.
4. Cut string into 12-inch pieces. (NOTE: You'll need 2 strings per tamale, about 82 strings.)
5. Using 2 or 3 husks, lay them rough side up, overlapping about 2 inches.
6. Using moistened hands, spread 2 tablespoons of prepared masa in the center of the husks, leaving at least 1 ½ inches of both ends empty.

7. Spread 2 tablespoons of meat over the masa.
8. Starting at one side, carefully roll the corn husks into a tube, keeping masa and meat inside.
9. Tie off ends securely with string, trimming excess ties.
10. Place about 10 tamales in a large metal colander or vegetable steamer. Place in a large pot and add water to a level just below the colander or steamer basket.
11. Cover securely and bring to a boil.
12. Steam tamales for 45–60 minutes, or until masa is firm and pulls away from the corn husks.
13. Repeat steps 10 through 12 for remaining tamales.
14. To make a chili gravy, bring remaining meat juice to a boil in a sauce pan.
15. Mix together cornstarch and water in a small bowl.
16. Whisk cornstarch mixture into boiling juice. Cook for 2–3 minutes to thicken, stirring frequently.
17. To serve tamales, remove husks and strings and discard. Pour chili gravy over the tamales.

Makes about 3 dozen.

SHREDDED BEEF TAQUITOS

2 ½ pounds 7-bone pot roast
1 (2 ½ ounce) package taco seasoning
2 cups water
½ cup vegetable oil
18 fresh corn tortillas

1. Cook meat with water and taco seasoning in a pressure cooker (35 minutes) or in medium crock pot (10 to 12 hours) until meat is very tender.
2. Remove meat to cool, reserving 2 cups of juice.
3. Shred meat into bite-size pieces.

4. Return meat to juice and simmer for 1 hour.
5. Soften tortillas by placing in a plastic bag and warming in a microwave on HIGH for 20 seconds OR by placing one tortilla at a time directly on a hot stove burner for 5 seconds on each side.
6. Heat oil in a heavy skillet over a high flame.
7. Place 2 to 3 tablespoons of meat down the center of a softened tortilla. Roll tortilla into a tube shape.
8. Place in the hot oil, loose-end side down first.
9. Fry until golden brown, then carefully turn taquito onto an uncooked side. Continue until all sides are browned.
10. Drain off excess oil.

Makes 6 servings.

PORK STEAKS WITH CHILE

1 pound pork steaks
1 tablespoon vegetable oil
¾ teaspoon salt
¼ teaspoon pepper
¼ teaspoon garlic powder
1 (10 ounce) can mild red chile sauce
½ cup water

1. In a skillet, heat oil over a medium flame.
2. Sprinkle both sides of the steaks evenly with salt, pepper, and garlic powder.
3. Place steaks in hot oil and brown both sides well.
4. Add chile sauce and water. Cover and bring to a boil.
5. Reduce heat and simmer for 40 minutes, or until the meat is tender when pierced by a fork.

Makes 4 servings.

NOPALITOS (CACTUS) AND CHILE

Grandma Lucy always used the fresh young cactus she grew in her garden, spending hours trimming away the prickly spines. We choose to use the kind that is already "despined" in jars!

—*J.H.*

.   1 (33 ounce) jar sliced cactus
2 tablespoons vegetable oil
¼ teaspoon garlic powder
1 (10 ounce) can red chile sauce
½ cup water
2 teaspoons cornstarch
2 tablespoons cold water
flour tortillas

1. Rinse cactus in a colander. Let drain.
2. In a large saucepan, heat oil over medium flame.
3. Add garlic powder and sauté until a golden brown.
4. Stir in chile sauce and water. Bring to a boil.
5. In a small bowl, whisk together cornstarch and water until smooth.
6. Whisk cornstarch mixture into chile sauce mixture. Cook 1 to 2 minutes to thicken, whisking occasionally.
7. Stir in cactus. Cook for 1 to 2 minutes to heat through.

Serve with tortillas.
Makes 4–5 servings.

NOPALITOS WITH EGGS

1 (33 ounce) jar sliced cactus
3 tablespoons vegetable oil
¼ cup chopped onion
8 eggs
⅛ teaspoon pepper
flour tortillas

1. Rinse cactus in a colander. Let drain.
2. In a large skillet, heat oil over medium flame.
3. Sauté onions in oil until soft and translucent.
4. Add cactus and heat through, stirring frequently.
5. In a bowl, beat eggs together lightly with pepper.
6. Add eggs to cactus and onion in the skillet and cook, stirring until eggs are cooked.

Serve with tortillas.
Makes 4–5 servings.

MEXICAN STEAK

1 pound chuck steak
¼ teaspoon garlic powder
¾ teaspoon salt
¼ teaspoon pepper
1 cup sliced onion
1 (16 ounce) can whole tomatoes (undrained and coarsely chopped)
1 (16 ounce) can whole kernel corn
½ cup diced mild green chiles

1. Heat oil in skillet over medium flame.
2. Sprinkle salt, pepper, and garlic powder evenly on both sides of steak.
3. Place meat in hot oil and brown one side of the steak.
4. When you flip the steak over to brown the other side, add onions and sauté until soft.
5. Stir in tomatoes, corn, and chiles. Cover and bring to a boil.
6. Reduce heat and simmer for 1 hour, or until meat is very tender.

Makes 4 servings.

MENUDO

Grandma Lucy sometimes served this soup-like dish for breakfast on Saturday and Sunday mornings. (It has a reputation for curing a hangover!)

3 pounds beef tripe
16 cups water, divided
3 beef bouillon cubes
1 ½ teaspoons salt
⅛ teaspoon pepper
¼ teaspoon crushed red pepper
¼ teaspoon garlic powder
1 (29 ounce) can white hominy

1. Wash tripe well.
2. Cut tripe into 1-inch square pieces, trimming off excess fatty tissue from back side (not the "honeycomb-looking" side.)
3. Place tripe pieces in a large kettle and cover with 8 cups of water.
4. Bring to a boil and continue boiling for 10 minutes.
5. Drain off water and rinse tripe pieces well.

6. Return tripe to kettle and add 8 cups fresh water.
7. Stir in bouillon cubes, salt, pepper, red pepper, and garlic powder.
8. Cover and bring to a boil.
9. Reduce heat and simmer for 30 minutes.
10. Drain hominy. Add to tripe mixture.
11. Cover and return to a boil.
12. Reduce heat and simmer for 1–2 hours, until tripe is tender.

Makes 6 servings.

BEEF TONGUE IN CHILE

Once considered a surplus cut of the beef, tongue is now thought to be a delicacy because of its leanness. I guess Great-Grandma Lucy was ahead of her time!

—J.G.

1 beef tongue (about 4 or 5 pounds)
3 tablespoons vegetable oil
¼ teaspoon garlic powder
1 (10 ounce) can red chile sauce
½ cup water
½ teaspoon salt
⅛ teaspoon pepper

1. Place tongue in large kettle and just cover with water.
2. Cover and bring to a boil.
3. Reduce heat just enough to keep water boiling. Cook for two hours, or until meat is very tender when pierced with a fork.
4. Remove meat from water and allow it to cool 15 minutes.
5. Remove any fat, bone, and the thick, whitish skin layer.
6. Dice meat into ½-inch pieces.

7. In a large saucepan, heat oil over medium flame.
8. Add garlic and sauté until golden brown.
9. Stir in chile sauce, water, salt, and pepper.
10. Bring to a boil.
11. Stir in meat and cook until meat is heated through.

Makes 5 servings.

CHILE RELLENOS

2 (7 ounce) cans whole green chiles
2 cups grated jack cheese
2 eggs, beaten
1 cup flour
1 teaspoon salt
⅛ teaspoon pepper
¼ cup vegetable oil

1. Carefully rinse chiles, trying not to split them. Remove seeds, if possible.
2. Divide cheese into piles equal to the number of chiles.
3. Carefully stuff cheese into open end of each chile.
4. Heat oil in a heavy skillet.
5. Place flour into a shallow pan. Mix in salt and pepper.
6. Dip stuffed chile into flour, then into beaten egg.
7. Lightly brown both sides of the chiles.
8. Drain excess oil on paper towels.

Makes about 4 servings.

FRIED MACARONI

This was Grandma Lucy's version of fideo, a Mexican-style macaroni soup.

—J.H.

1 tablespoon vegetable oil
2 ½ cups salad macaroni, uncooked
½ teaspoon garlic powder
4 cups water
1 (8 ounce) can tomato sauce
½ teaspoon salt
⅛ teaspoon pepper
1 cup grated cheddar cheese

1. In a large skillet, heat oil over a medium flame.
2. Stir in macaroni and garlic powder and brown macaroni to a golden color.
3. Stir in water, tomato sauce, salt, and pepper.
4. Cover and bring to a boil.
5. Reduce heat and simmer for 10–15 minutes, or until macaroni is tender.
6. Stir in cheese and remove from heat.
7. Let stand 5 minutes before serving.

Makes 6 servings.

STEAK AND RICE

1 pound chuck steak
2 tablespoons vegetable oil
1 cup rice, uncooked
¼ teaspoon garlic powder

1 (8 ounce) can tomato sauce
2 ½ cups water
¾ teaspoon salt
⅛ teaspoon pepper

1. Cut away any bone or excess fat. Tenderize if desired.
2. Cut meat into half-inch cubes.
3. Sauté meat and garlic in oil until the meat loses its pink color.
4. Stir in rice and cook until rice is golden brown.
5. Stir in tomato sauce, water, salt, and pepper.
6. Bring to a boil. Cover and reduce heat.
7. Simmer for 30 minutes or until rice is tender.

Makes 5 servings.

STEAK AND POTATO CASSEROLE

2 pounds chuck steak (bone-in)
2 teaspoons meat tenderizer
5 or 6 medium potatoes
1 (16 ounce) can whole peeled tomatoes
1 tablespoon vegetable oil
1 cup thinly-sliced onions
1 (4 ounce) can diced mild green chiles
1 ½ teaspoons salt
¼ teaspoon pepper

1. Preheat oven to 350 degrees.
2. Remove excess fat from the meat.
3. Moisten meat with water and sprinkle meat tenderizer evenly on both sides. Pierce with a fork.
4. Peel and slice potatoes into ¼-inch slices.
5. In a small bowl, break tomatoes into coarse chunks.
6. Pour oil in the bottom of a 4 quart casserole dish.

7. Layer half of the following ingredients in this order: meat, onion, potatoes, tomatoes, chiles, salt, and pepper.
8. Repeat for the second layer.
9. Cover tightly with a lid or foil.
10. Bake for 1 ½ hours, or until meat is cooked through and potatoes are tender.

Makes 5 servings.

VEGETABLE BEEF SOUP

Grandma Lucy served this soup every Sunday. It was a light meal in contrast to the heavy, hearty meals she made the other days for her hard-working family. She said it gave their stomachs and her kitchen a much-needed rest.

—J.H.

1 (2 ½ pound) 7 bone roast
1 medium onion, sliced
15 cups water
2 ½ teaspoons salt
½ teaspoon pepper
½ garlic powder
1 ½ cups sliced carrots
1 ½ cups green beans
2 cups whole kernel corn OR 4 ears fresh corn, cut into thirds
1 ½ cups sliced celery
4 medium potatoes, peeled and cut into cubes
2 zucchini, sliced
1 small head cabbage, cut into eighths

1. In a large pot, place roast, onion, water, salt, pepper, and garlic powder.
2. Cover and bring to a boil.

3. Reduce heat slightly and let cook at a slow boil for 2 hours, or until meat is very tender.
4. Remove meat from the pot, reserving stock.
5. Remove and discard any fat or bone.
6. Shred meat into bite-sized pieces.
7. Return meat to stock.
8. Cover and return to a boil.
9. Stir in carrots, green beans, corn, and celery.
10. Cover and return to a boil.
11. Reduce heat slightly and cook for 45–60 minutes, or until vegetables are tender but firm.
12. Stir in potatoes, zucchini, and cabbage.
13. Cover and return to a boil.
14. Reduce heat slightly and cook for 20 minutes, or until potatoes, zucchini, and cabbage are tender.

Makes 8–10 servings.

SAUCY HOT DOGS

½ pound hot dogs
2 teaspoons vegetable oil
2 tablespoons chopped onions
½ cup tomato sauce
¼ cup water
1 ½ tablespoons diced mild green chiles

1. Cut hot dogs into ¼-inch slices.
2. Put slices into a skillet with oil and onion.
3. Over a medium flame, cook until onions are golden brown, stirring frequently.
4. Add tomato sauce, water, and chiles.
5. Bring to a boil.
6. Reduce heat and simmer, uncovered, for 10 minutes.

Makes 2 servings.

MEXICAN SAUTÉED SPINACH

Grandma Lucy often wrapped this vegetable dish in a tortilla and included it in her family's workday lunch.

—*J.H.*

2 pounds fresh spinach
1 ½ tablespoons oil
⅛ teaspoon garlic powder
¼ teaspoon salt
1 ½ tablespoons flour
½ cup grated cheddar OR jack cheese

1. Wash spinach well.
2. Steam until just tender. Cool.
3. Squeeze out excess water. Drain well.
4. Chop spinach into small pieces.
5. In a skillet, heat oil over a low flame.
6. Add spinach, garlic powder, and salt, stirring occasionally.
7. Sauté for 5 minutes.
8. Stir in flour until well mixed.
9. Sauté for another 5 minutes.
10. Add cheese, stirring until melted and blended.

Makes 4 servings.

SUMMER SQUASH AND CHEESE

2 ½ pounds summer squash
3 tablespoons vegetable oil

¼ teaspoon garlic powder
½ teaspoon salt
1 ¼ cups grated cheddar cheese
flour tortillas

1. Trim off stem and any bruised parts of the squash. (NOTE: Do not peel.)
2. Rinse and drain squash well.
3. Cut into 1-inch chunks.
4. Heat oil in a skillet over a medium flame.
5. Add squash and garlic, stirring occasionally until squash is lightly browned and tender.
6. Gently stir in cheese.
7. Cover and remove from the heat.
8. Let stand 5 minutes, then stir gently to blend in melted cheese.

Serve with flour tortillas.
Makes 5 servings.

————————

SPICY FRIED RICE

2 tablespoons vegetable oil
1 ½ cups rice, uncooked
⅛ teaspoon garlic powder
¼ teaspoon ground cumin
1 teaspoon chopped fresh cilantro
1 cup fresh tomato salsa #2 (see page 32)
3 cups water
1 teaspoon salt

1. Heat oil in a skillet over a medium flame.
2. Add rice, garlic powder, cumin, and cilantro. Stir until rice is golden brown.

3. Add salsa, water, and salt. Cover and bring to a boil.
4. Reduce heat and simmer for 20 minutes, or until rice has absorbed the moisture.

Makes 6 servings.

PLAIN FRIED RICE

2 cups uncooked long-grain rice
⅓ cup vegetable oil
¾ teaspoon garlic powder
2 teaspoons salt
¼ teaspoon pepper
4 ½ cups water

1. Heat oil in a large skillet over medium flame.
2. Add rice and garlic powder. Stir until rice is lightly browned.
3. Add water, salt, and pepper.
4. Cover pan and bring to a boil.
5. Reduce heat and simmer for 20 minutes, or until rice is tender and the water is absorbed.

Makes 7 cups.

FLOUR TORTILLAS

When Mom married Dad, she learned how to cook the foods he liked from Grandma Lucy. Since tortillas were a staple, she started with this one. However, Mom couldn't seem to stretch them as round or as large as Grandma Lucy could,

*but she didn't want to admit it. So she went home "to practice"
and instead, rolled them into whatever shape she could, then
placed a dinner plate over them and cut them out. For months,
Grandma Lucy was very proud of her new daughter-in-law's
skill, until she happened to pass by Mom's window one day
and caught her in the act!*

—*J.H.*

5 cups flour
2 teaspoons salt
¾ cup vegetable shortening
1 ⅔ cups lukewarm water
1 cup flour
Extra flour, as needed

1. Using a pastry blender or fork, mix together 5 cups flour, salt, and vegetable shortening until crumbly.
2. Slowly mix in water well until dough is soft and sticks together. (NOTE: Using your hands to mix seems to work the best. Also, you may need a little more flour OR a little more water to reach a soft dough.)
3. Turn dough out onto a floured board. Knead for 7–8 minutes, adding a little more flour to board if the dough starts to stick.
4. Pinch off golf-ball sized pieces of dough and roll into a ball.
5. Place balls on a lightly-floured board and cover the board and balls with plastic wrap to keep out as much air as possible. Let stand for 50 minutes.
6. Heat an ungreased griddle or large cast-iron skillet until a drop of water will "dance" on it.
7. While the griddle or pan is heating, place 1 cup flour in a shallow bowl. One at a time, place dough ball in the flour and flatten both sides until it is a thick circle, about 4 inches across.
8. On a floured board, use a rolling pin to roll out each ball into a thin, flattened circle, about 10 inches across.

9. Gently pick up the tortilla and pull and stretch outward from the center. Finished size will vary, depending on your ability to pull consistently. (NOTE: See story at the beginning of the recipe!)
10. Lay tortilla on heated griddle. Cook until bubbles form and are lightly browned on bottom. Flip with a spatula.
11. Cook other side until lightly browned.
12. Remove and stack on a platter or cake pan for storage.

Store covered.

These can be rewarmed by laying them briefly on your stove's flame or burner for a few seconds per side.

Makes about 2 dozen.

FRESH TOMATO SALSA 1

5 medium tomatoes
4 cups boiling water
4 cups cold tap water
½ cup onion, chopped
1 (4 ounce) can diced green chiles (mild)
½ teaspoon salt

1. Place tomatoes in a large bowl.
2. Pour boiling water over tomatoes to cover.
3. Let tomatoes stand in the water for 3 minutes.
4. Drain off hot water, then pour cold water over the tomatoes. Let stand for 1 minute.
5. Drain off water.
6. Peel skins from the tomatoes. Chop peeled tomatoes into coarse chunks and place in a medium-sized bowl.
7. Add onions, chiles, and salt. Gently toss together to mix.
8. Cover tightly and chill for at least 1 hour.

Makes about 3 cups.

FRESH TOMATO SALSA 2

6 medium tomatoes
½ cup chopped fresh cilantro (a Mexican leafy herb)
1 teaspoon salt
¼ cup water
1 teaspoon bottled hot sauce

1. Remove cores from tomatoes, then quarter.
2. Place all ingredients into a blender.
3. Blend until smooth.
4. Refrigerate 1 hour before serving.

Makes about 3 cups.

CHEESE SAUCE

Grandma Lucy served this rich, creamy sauce with rice and beans. I have found it to be a great dip for chips and vegetables, as well.

—*J.G.*

2 ½ tablespoons vegetable oil
½ cup finely chopped onion
1 (15 ounce) can whole tomatoes
¼ teaspoon crushed red pepper
8 ounces Velveeta cheese, cut into 1-inch cubes

1. In a sauce pan, sauté onions in oil until soft and golden brown.
2. In a small bowl, cut tomatoes into coarse pieces.
3. Add tomatoes to sautéed onions.

4. Stir in crushed red peppers.
5. Bring to a boil. Reduce heat and let simmer uncovered for 40 minutes.
6. Add cheese to the onion and tomato mixture. Stir until cheese melts.

Makes 2 cups.

GUACAMOLE

2 ripe avocados
⅛ teaspoon garlic powder
2 tablespoons fresh salsa
½ teaspoon lemon juice
2 tablespoons mayonnaise
½ teaspoon salt

1. Peel away avocado skins.
2. Remove pits and save.*
3. Place avocado meat, garlic powder, salsa, lemon juice, mayonnaise, and salt in a blender.
4. Blend until smooth.

Makes about 2 cups.

*If you are serving at a later time, place avocado pits back into the guacamole and store in the refrigerator. They will keep the guacamole from turning brown. Remember to remove pits before serving.

PICKLED CARROTS

Grandma Lucy spent many hours tending a vegetable garden behind her home. I can still see her out there in her big, floppy hat and gloves, pulling vegetables for her meals. This recipe was an easy favorite.

6 medium carrots
¼ cup vinegar
½ cup vegetable oil
½ teaspoon salt
½ teaspoon crushed red chiles
¼ teaspoon garlic powder

1. Peel and cut carrots into julienne strips.
2. Place carrots into a large sauce pan and cover with water. Bring to a boil.
3. Cook carrots until tender but firm. Drain off excess water.
4. In a medium bowl with a tight-fitting lid, mix together vinegar, oil, salt, crushed red chiles, and garlic powder.
5. Add carrots to mixture and toss well.
6. Cover tightly and refrigerate for at least 4 hours, mixing occasionally to allow flavors to blend evenly.

Makes 4-6 servings.

CORN AND CHILE MEDLEY

2 medium tomatoes
4 cups boiling water
4 cups cold tap water
1 pound (4 cups) frozen whole-kernel corn
2 tablespoons diced green chiles
4 tablespoons chopped onions

1. Place tomatoes in a large bowl.
2. Pour boiling water over tomatoes to cover completely. Let stand for 3 minutes.
3. Drain off hot water then add cold water and let stand for 1 minute.
4. Drain off water.
5. Peel skin from tomatoes. Chop peeled tomatoes into coarse chunks. Set aside.
6. Thaw corn according to package directions. Set aside.
7. In medium sauce pan, heat vegetable oil. Add onions and sauté until just soft.
8. Add tomatoes and chiles and sauté for 2-3 minutes.
9. Add corn. Bring to a boil.
10. Cover and reduce heat. Simmer for 10 minutes.

Makes 6 servings.

RICE PUDDING

Desserts weren't always served, since the meals were very filling. But when someone had a "sweet tooth," Grandma Lucy would put together this healthy dish.

—J.H.

1 cup uncooked rice
4 cups milk
½ cup raisins
dash of salt
1 teaspoon vanilla
ground cinnamon

1. Place rice, milk, raisins and salt in a sauce pan.
2. Bring to a boil, then cover and reduce heat.
3. Simmer for 30 to 40 minutes, or until milk is absorbed and rice is tender.

4. Remove from heat and stir in vanilla.
5. Serve warm or cooled. Sprinkle cinnamon on top before serving.

Makes 4 servings.

PLAIN WHITE CAKE

I lived next door to my Grandma Lucy during my child-hood. Often, I would go over and she'd say, "Let's make a cake!" In a flash she'd have the batter for this cake together and in the oven. Then we would enjoy it warm with jelly spread on the top. My favorite was grape!

—J.H.

2 cups flour
3 teaspoons baking powder
½ teaspoon salt
½ cup butter OR margarine, melted
1 cup sugar
2 eggs
¾ cups milk
1 teaspoon vanilla

1. Preheat oven to 350 degrees.
2. Grease and flour a 5 X 9-inch loaf pan.
3. In a medium bowl, combine flour, baking powder, and salt. Set aside.
4. In a large bowl, stir together melted butter OR margarine, sugar, eggs, milk, and vanilla until just blended.
5. Gradually stir in flour mixture until dry ingredients are just moistened.
6. Pour batter into prepared pan.
7. Bake for 55–60 minutes, or until a toothpick comes out clean and dry.

8. Cool in pan for 10 minutes.
9. Remove from pan and cool on a wire rack.

Serve warm or cooled, plain or with fruit jam spread on top.
Makes 1 loaf.

ORANGE TOAST

*Grandma Lucy often put together this fruity breakfast
dish, but she never made this breakfast or any other until she
was all put together herself; dressed, with make-up and hair
all impeccably done.*

—*J.H.*

2 oranges
4 slices white bread
4 teaspoons butter OR margarine
4 tablespoons brown sugar

1. Peel oranges, removing as much of the whitish part of the peel as possible.
2. Slice orange into ¼-inch slices.
3. Toast one side of bread slices in the broiler.
4. Remove from broiler and spread 1 teaspoon butter OR margarine on untoasted side.
5. Sprinkle 1 tablespoon of brown sugar over butter OR margarine.
6. Arrange enough orange slices to cover the bread in a single layer.
7. Repeat steps 4 through 6 for the remaining 3 slices of bread.
8. Return to the broiler, orange side up, and broil for 2–2 ½ minutes, watching carefully so as not to burn it.

Makes 4 servings.

DOWN-HOME DISHES

DOWN-HOME FAMILY MATRIARCH
OPAL HOLSTEN

WHITE BEANS WITH HAM HOCKS

Grandma Opal often said she "set up a pot of beans" to take the chill off a cold winter day.

—J.G.

1 ½ cups small dried white beans*
1–1 ½ pounds meaty ham hock
7 cups water**
1 tablespoon dried onion OR 1 medium onion, chopped
¼ teaspoon salt
¼ teaspoon pepper

1. Wash beans, removing any stones or debris.
2. Place beans in a large kettle.
3. Add ham hock, water, onion, salt, and pepper.
4. Cover and bring to a boil.
5. Reduce heat and simmer for 3 hours, or until beans are tender.

Makes 6-8 servings.

*2 cups Lima beans can be substituted for white beans.
**If preparing Lima beans, use 8 cups of water.

LIVER AND ONIONS

1 pound beef liver
¾ teaspoon salt
⅛ teaspoon pepper
2 tablespoons vegetable oil
1 ½ cups sliced onion
1 cup water

1. Cut liver into serving-size pieces.
2. Sprinkle salt and pepper evenly on both sides of the meat.
3. Heat oil in a skillet over a medium flame.
4. Place liver in the hot oil. Brown both sides and remove from the skillet.
5. Place onions in oil/liver drippings. Place browned liver on top of the onions. Carefully stir occasionally until onions are lightly browned.
6. Leaving meat on top of the onions, add water to the skillet. Cover and bring to a boil.
7. Reduce heat and simmer for 1 hour.

Makes 4 servings.

MEATBALLS AND GRAVY

1 ½ pounds hamburger
½ cup finely chopped onion
1 teaspoon salt
¼ teaspoon pepper
3 tablespoons vegetable oil
1 cup water
2 ½ cups milk
¼ cup flour
½ cup cold water
½ teaspoon salt
⅛ teaspoon pepper

1. Mix hamburger, onion, 1 teaspoon salt and ¼ teaspoon pepper together thoroughly. Form into golf ball-size meatballs.
2. Heat oil in a skillet over low flame.
3. Brown meatballs well on all sides.
4. Remove meatballs from skillet and place on paper towels to absorb excess oil.
5. Pour off most of oil and drippings from skillet, leaving approximately 2 tablespoons.
6. Over low flame, stir and loosen drippings from pan, and brown any remaining onions.
7. Add milk and 1 cup water to drippings. Bring to a boil.
8. In a small container with a lid (a jar works well) shake together ½ cup cold water and ¼ cup flour.
9. Slowly pour flour/water mixture into drippings, stirring constantly until thickened.
10. Stir in ½ teaspoon salt and ⅛ teaspoon pepper. Return meatballs to pan with gravy.
11. Cover and simmer for 30 minutes. Then remove lid and continue simmering for another 15 minutes.

Serve over mashed potatoes, noodles, or rice.
Makes 6 servings.

POTATO AND HAMBURGER CASSEROLE

This has always been one of my favorites that Opal taught me; not just for its great taste but because it is so easy to make.
—J.H.

1 ½ pounds hamburger
1 (10 ¾) ounce can condensed cream of mushroom soup
    OR condensed cream of celery soup
1 cup water
1 teaspoon salt, divided

¼ teaspoon pepper, divided
6 medium potatoes, peeled and sliced into ⅛-inch slices
(approximately 5 cups sliced potatoes)
2 cups grated cheddar cheese

1. Brown hamburger in a skillet, breaking into coarse chunks. Drain off excess fat. Divide.
2. In a small bowl, mix together condensed soup and water.
3. In a 12 X 8-inch ungreased pan, layer half of each ingredient in this order: sliced potatoes, hamburger, salt, pepper, cheese, soup mixture. Repeat for second layer.
4. Cover pan tightly with foil.
5. Bake at 350 degrees for 1 hour 15 minutes or until potatoes are tender when pierced by a fork.
6. Remove foil and bake for another 10 minutes.

Makes 8 servings.

POTATO SOUP

6 medium potatoes
1 large onion, quartered
7 cups water
1 cup milk
¼ cup margarine, melted
1 ½ teaspoons salt
⅛ teaspoon pepper

1. Peel potatoes and cut into thick chunks.
2. Place potatoes, onion, and water into a large pot.
3. Cover and bring to a boil.
4. Reduce heat slightly and let cook at a slow boil for 30–40 minutes, or until potatoes and onions are very soft.
5. Remove potatoes and onion, reserving 2 cups of the water in the pot.

6. Puree potatoes and onion in a blender or food processor until smooth.
7. Return pureed mixture to water in the pot. Stir in milk and margarine.
8. Heat through and serve.

Makes 6 servings.

DOWN HOME MEATLOAF

1 ½ pounds hamburger
½ cup finely chopped celery
½ cup chopped bell pepper
½ cup grated carrot
½ cup chopped onion
1 teaspoon salt
¼ teaspoon garlic powder
1 (8 ounce) can tomato sauce
2 eggs
25 squares soda crackers, crushed

1. Mix all ingredients together well.
2. Form into a loaf and place in an ungreased baking pan.
3. Bake at 350 degrees for 1 ½ hours.

Makes 6 servings.

BEEF STEW

1 pound stewing beef
⅓ cup flour
⅓ cup vegetable oil
4 cups water
1 ½ tablespoons dry onion

2 teaspoons salt
¼ teaspoon pepper
2 ½ cups potatoes, peeled and cut into 2-inch cubes.
2 cups carrots, peeled and cut into 1/2 inch slices
1 beef bouillon cube
½ cup water
2 ½ teaspoons flour

1. Cut meat into 2-inch square pieces.
2. Coat meat lightly with ⅓ cup flour.
3. In a large kettle or pot, heat oil over medium flame.
4. Add meat to heated oil and brown well.
5. Add 4 cups water, dry onion, salt, and pepper.
6. Bring to a full boil, scraping the bottom of the pan to loosen any meat dripping.
7. Cover and reduce to a low flame. Simmer for 1 ½ hours, or until the meat is tender.
8. Add carrots and continue simmering until carrots are just tender.
9. Add potatoes and continue simmering until potatoes are just tender.
10. Add bouillon cube.
11. In a small bowl, mix together ½ cup water and 2 ½ teaspoons flour. Add to the stew and stir in well. Cook for 5 minutes over medium flame, stirring occasionally.

Makes 8 servings.

CHICKEN POT PIE

Opal helped run a small diner in her younger days. ("I was chief cook and bottle washer!") This was one of her customers' favorites.

—J.H.

1 ½–2 pounds chicken with skin and bones
3 cups water
10 ounces fresh OR frozen mixed vegetables (corn, peas, carrot slices, cut green beans, etc.)
1 ½ cups potatoes, peeled and cubed
1 teaspoon seasoned salt
¼ teaspoon garlic powder
⅛ teaspoon pepper
1 (10 ¾) ounce can condensed cream of chicken soup
2 tablespoons water
double pie crust to line and cover 8 X 8-inch baking pan

1. In a large kettle, place chicken pieces, 4 cups water, seasoned salt, garlic powder, and pepper.
2. Cover and bring to a full boil. Reduce to low flame and cook for 30 minutes, or until chicken is tender.
3. Remove chicken from the pot, reserving broth. Set chicken aside to cool.
4. Bring broth to a gentle boil.
5. Add mixed vegetables and potatoes. Cook until potatoes are tender.
6. Add soup to broth mixture, stirring until well blended.
7. Reduce flame and simmer 5 minutes.
8. Remove skin and bones from cooled chicken and discard. Cut chicken meat into bite-sized pieces.
9. Add chicken pieces to broth mixture.
10. Bring to a boil.
11. In a small bowl, combine cornstarch and 2 tablespoons water. Stir until smooth.
12. Add cornstarch mixture to chicken mixture, stirring well.
13. Reduce heat and simmer for 5 minutes until thickened.
14. Line an 8 X 8-inch baking pan with one pie crust, making sure the sides are covered.
15. Pour in chicken mixture.
16. Cover pan with the remaining pie crust, sealing edges well. Cut 3 or 4 slits in the top.
17. Bake at 350 degrees for 30 minutes, or until top crust is golden brown.

Makes 6 servings.

CHILE MACARONI CASSEROLE

Opal often made this as a company dish because it could be baking while she "visited," one of her favorite pastimes!
—*J.H.*

1 pound hamburger
2 teaspoons chili powder
1 (6 ounce) can tomato paste
2 ½ cups water
1 tablespoon dry onion
1 ½ teaspoons salt
⅛ teaspoon pepper
3 ½ cups large elbow macaroni, uncooked
2 ½ cups grated cheddar cheese

1. Brown hamburger, breaking into coarse chunks. Drain off excess grease.
2. Stir in chili powder, tomato paste, water, onion, salt, and pepper. Mix well.
3. Bring hamburger mixture to a boil. Reduce heat and simmer uncovered for 15 minutes.
4. Cook macaroni according to package directions. Drain and place in an 11 X 7-inch casserole dish.
5. Mix about 1 cup of the hamburger mixture into the macaroni to coat.
6. Spoon remaining hamburger mixture evenly over the macaroni.
7. Sprinkle grated cheese over the hamburger mixture. Bake uncovered for 20 minutes at 400 degrees or until cheese is melted.

Makes 6 servings.

BUTTERMILK CHICKEN

Opal's version of fried chicken is so moist and tender!
—J.H.

8 pieces of chicken (legs, thighs, or breasts)
1 cup buttermilk
1 cup flour
2 teaspoons salt
¼ teaspoon pepper
⅓ cup vegetable oil

1. Mix flour, salt, and pepper together in a shallow bowl. Set aside.
2. Pour buttermilk into a separate shallow bowl.
3. Dredge chicken in flour mixture well, shaking off excess.
4. Dip flour-covered chicken in the buttermilk.
5. Dip again in the flour mixture.
6. Heat oil in a heavy skillet over a medium-high flame.
7. Place chicken in hot oil, browning each side quickly. (NOTE: Chicken will not be cooked through at this point.)
8. Place chicken on an ungreased baking sheet and cover tightly with foil.
9. Bake at 350 degrees for 30 minutes, or until chicken is tender and cooked through.
10. Remove foil and continue baking for 10 minutes more.

Makes 8 servings.

BEEF AND NOODLES

1 ½ pounds stewing beef
½ cup flour
¼ cup vegetable oil
4 cups water

2 teaspoons salt
¼ teaspoon pepper
1 ½ tablespoons dry onion
12 ounces noodles, uncooked

1. Cut meat into 1-inch pieces.
2. Coat meat with flour.
3. In a large kettle or pot, heat oil over a medium-high flame.
4. Add coated meat to hot oil, stirring frequently until meat is well browned.
5. Add water, salt, pepper, and dry onion.
6. Bring to a boil. Cover and reduce heat.
7. Simmer for 1 ½ hours, or until meat is tender. Remove from heat.
8. Cook noodles according to package directions. Drain.
9. Add noodles to meat, stirring well.
10. Cover and let stand 15 minutes to let noodles absorb some of the liquid. Stir occasionally.

Makes 6 servings.

———— •·• ————

STUFFED BELL PEPPERS

5 large bell peppers
¾ pound hamburger
¾ cup rice, uncooked
⅛ teaspoon garlic powder
1 (8 ounce) can tomato sauce
3 cups water
1 tablespoon dry minced onion
1 teaspoon salt
⅛ teaspoon pepper
1 ¼ cups grated jack cheese

1. Clean bell peppers by cutting off tops and removing seeds, rinsing well.
2. Steam bell peppers until tender but not soft.
3. Place in a casserole dish and set aside.
4. Brown hamburger. Drain off all but 1 tablespoon of drippings.
5. Add rice and garlic powder to hamburger. Continue cooking just to lightly brown rice.
6. Stir in tomato sauce, water, onion, salt, and pepper.
7. Cover and bring to a boil.
8. Reduce heat and simmer for 30 minutes, or until rice is tender and liquid absorbed.
9. Spoon hamburger/rice mixture evenly into bell peppers.
10. Cover and bake at 325 degrees for 30 minutes.
11. Sprinkle cheese evenly over top of bell peppers and bake, uncovered, for 5 minutes to melt cheese.

Makes 5 servings.

BREADED PORK CHOPS AND RICE

1 egg
½ teaspoon salt
¼ teaspoon pepper
1 cup finely-crushed saltine crackers
3 thick-cut pork chops
6 tablespoons vegetable oil
1 cup rice, uncooked
¼ teaspoon garlic powder
2 ¼ cups water
1 teaspoon salt
¼ teaspoon pepper

1. In a shallow bowl, beat together egg, salt, and pepper.

2. Spread cracker crumbs on a length of waxed paper.
3. Dip chops in beaten egg mixture, then press firmly in cracker crumbs, coating completely.
4. In a heavy skillet, heat oil, over a medium flame.
5. Place breaded chops in hot oil, browning both sides well. (NOTE: Chops will not be cooked through at this point.)
6. Remove meat, reserving drippings.
7. Lightly grease a 7 X 11-inch baking dish.
8. Place chops in the dish. Cover tightly with foil.
9. Bake at 325 degrees for 90 minutes, or until chops are tender and cooked through.
10. To make rice, add rice and garlic powder to chop drippings.
11. Over a medium flame, brown rice to a golden color, stirring frequently.
12. Stir in water, salt, and pepper.
13. Cover and bring to a boil.
14. Reduce heat and simmer 20 minutes, or until rice is tender and water is absorbed.

Makes 3 servings.

FRIED BEEF STRIPS

3 pounds round steak
1 cup flour
1 teaspoon salt
¼ teaspoon pepper
⅓ cup vegetable oil

1. Trim excess fat from the round steak.
2. Cut beef into thin slices, approximately 1/8 inch thick. Set aside.
3. Place flour, salt, and pepper into a large plastic bag. Close off opening and shake ingredients together well.

4. Place several pieces of meat into flour mixture. Close off opening and shake well to dredge meat pieces.
5. Heat oil in heavy skillet over high flame.
6. Quickly brown meat strips in hot oil. Remove pieces and place on paper towels to drain off excess oil.
7. Season meat to taste with salt and pepper.

Serve with rice or mashed potatoes.
Makes 5 servings.

STOVE-TOP POT ROAST AND GRAVY

Opal made this for us when we visited. It quickly became a much-requested meal at our house.

—J.H.

¼ cup vegetable oil
1 teaspoon salt, divided
½ teaspoon pepper, divided
1 teaspoon garlic powder, divided
3 pounds boneless chuck roast or 7-bone roast
3 cups water
2 tablespoons cornstarch
¼ cup water

1. In a heavy skillet, heat oil over medium-high flame.
2. Sprinkle half of salt, pepper, and garlic powder evenly over the meat. Place this side down in the oil.
3. Sprinkle remaining salt, pepper, and garlic powder on top of meat. Cover and brown both sides of meat very well.
4. Add 3 cups water, cover and bring to boil.
5. Reduce heat and simmer for 1 ½ hours, or until meat is very tender.
6. Remove meat from pan, set aside.
7. Bring pan drippings to boil.

8. In a small container with a tight-fitting lid, shake together cornstarch and ¼ cup water. Add to pan, stirring well to mix thoroughly.
9. Reduce heat and continue to stir until gravy thickens. Return meat to pan and allow to simmer in the gravy for 10 minutes.

Serve with mashed potatoes or rice.
Makes 6 servings.

CORNED BEEF HASH

6–7 medium potatoes, peeled
1 can (12 ounce) corned beef*
2 tablespoons vegetable oil
½ cup thinly sliced onions
2 cups water**
⅛ teaspoon pepper

1. Slice potatoes into approximately 1/4-inch slices.
2. In a heavy skillet, heat vegetable oil over high flame until hot.
3. Add potatoes and cover skillet with lid. Stir occasionally until potatoes are lightly browned. (NOTE: potatoes will not be cooked through at this point.)
4. Add onions and stir occasionally until onions soften.
5. In a bowl, break up corned beef into smaller chunks.
6. Add corned beef to potato and onions, stirring to warm the meat.
7. Add water and pepper. Bring to a boil, then cover and reduce heat.
8. Simmer for 40 minutes, or until most of the water is absorbed and potatoes are tender.

Makes 5 servings.
*Can use 2 cups shredded leftover roast beef in place of corned beef.
**Can mix one can (8 ounce) tomato sauce to the water for a slightly tangy taste.

RED CORNED BEEF WITH RICE

½ cup thinly sliced onions
1 (12 ounce) can corned beef
1 (8 ounce) can tomato sauce
2 tablespoons oil
1 ½ cups water
1 cup uncooked rice

1. Sauté onions in oil until soft.
2. Add corned beef, tomato sauce, and water. Stir together, breaking up corned beef.
3. Cover and bring to a boil. Reduce heat and simmer for 5 minutes.
4. Prepare rice according to package directions.
5. Serve red corned beef over the rice.

Makes 4 servings.

BEEF DIPS

3 pounds rump roast
5 cups water
¾ teaspoon salt
1 teaspoon garlic powder
½ teaspoon pepper
6 French rolls, split

1. Place roast in a roasting pan or large casserole dish with a tight-fitting lid.
2. Pour in water.
3. Sprinkle salt, garlic powder, and pepper over meat and water.

4. Cover and roast at 300 degrees for 2 ½ to 3 hours, or until meat is tender.
5. Remove meat, reserving juice.
6. Cool meat then slice thinly.
7. Spoon juice over opened French rolls. Pile meat on the bread.

Makes 6 servings—with plenty of meat left over for another meal!

BARBECUED BEEF SANDWICHES

1 pound lean stewing beef
2 tablespoons vegetable oil
1 cup sliced onion
1 cup prepared barbecue sauce
½ cup water
6 sandwich rolls or buns

1. Trim excess fat and gristle from meat.
2. Heat oil in a heavy skillet over a medium flame.
3. Add beef and onion slices to hot oil. Brown meat and onions, stirring occasionally. Meat should be just cooked through.
4. Using a food processor or blender, shred meat and onion into small pieces. (NOTE: Be careful not to overshred into a mush!)
5. Put shredded meat and onion mixture back into the skillet.
6. Stir in barbecue sauce and simmer, uncovered, for 10 minutes.
7. Serve over rolls or buns.

Makes 6 servings.

BOLOGNA CUP SANDWICHES

Opal made these quick lunch treats, and I think my family requested them almost daily for a month!

—*J.H.*

4 slices thick-cut bologna
1 teaspoon vegetable oil
4 hamburger buns
4 eggs
ketchup

1. In a skillet, heat oil over medium flame.
2. Brown bologna in hot oil until it starts to curl up into a cup shape.
3. Remove and place on paper toweling to remove excess oil.
4. In a bowl, slightly beat eggs.
5. Place eggs in skillet and cook as scrambled eggs.
6. Place one bologna cup on one half of each hamburger bun.
7. Divide eggs into 4 equal portions and spoon into bologna cups.
8. Top with ketchup and cover with other half of bun.

Makes 4 servings.

GRANDMA'S GREEN BEANS

Grandma Opal had the largest hands I had ever seen on a woman. But I remember watching her, just mesmerized, as her experienced fingers flew with grace to snap the fresh green beans from her garden.

—*J.G.*

2 pounds fresh green beans
¼ pound sliced bacon
½ teaspoon salt
¼ teaspoon pepper
2 cups water

1. Clean and snap green beans into 1-inch pieces.
2. Place all ingredients in a large covered pot or kettle.
3. Bring to a boil. Stir and reduce to lowest possible flame and return cover.
4. Cook for 3 hours, stirring occasionally to break up bacon into small pieces.

Makes 5 servings.

SCALLOPED CORN CASSEROLE

CASSEROLE:
2 (16 ounce) cans cream-style corn
2 eggs, slightly beaten
¼ cup sugar
¼ cup margarine, melted
¼ teaspoon salt
⅛ teaspoon pepper
24 saltine crackers, crushed

TOPPING:
6 saltine crackers, crushed
1 teaspoon paprika

1. Combine corn, eggs, sugar, margarine, salt, pepper, and 24 crushed crackers. Mix well.
2. Pour into a greased 8 X 8-inch casserole dish.
3. Mix together 6 crushed crackers and paprika. Sprinkle evenly over corn mixture.
4. Bake for 50 minutes, or until a knife inserted in the middle comes out clean.
5. Remove from oven and allow to stand for 10 minutes before serving.

Makes 6 servings.

BAKED BEANS

When Opal first served these rich beans, I felt guilty. I just knew she must have spent hours in the kitchen. It wasn't until after dinner that she let me in on her secret—it only took 10 minutes to prepare, and the oven did the rest of the work!

—J.H.

1 (30 ounce) can pork and beans
AND
1 (15 ounce) can pork and beans
½ cup catsup
3 tablespoons molasses
½ cup onion, chopped
¼ cup brown sugar
3 slices bacon, uncooked

1. Drain excess liquid from beans, discarding any large pieces of pork fat.
2. Place beans in a 2-quart baking dish.
3. Add catsup, molasses, onion, brown sugar, and bacon slices. Stir together to mix.
4. Bake uncovered at 350 degrees for 2 hours.

Makes 6 servings.

AMBROSIA FRUIT SALAD

1 (20 ounce) can fruit cocktail
1 (16 ounce) can chunk pineapple
2 cups miniature marshmallows
¾ cup flaked coconut
8 ounces sour cream

1. Drain off half of the juice from both cans of fruit.
2. Place fruit with half of juice in a large bowl.
3. Stir in marshmallows.
4. Cover and chill for 1 hour, stirring occasionally.
5. Stir in coconut and sour cream.
6. Cover and chill for at least 1 hour before serving.

Makes 8 servings.

CREAMED POTATOES

4 medium potatoes
4 tablespoons butter OR margarine
2 cups milk
3 tablespoons flour
¾ teaspoon salt
⅛ teaspoon pepper

1. Peel potatoes and cut into large chunks.
2. Place in pot and just cover with water.
3. Cover and bring to a boil.
4. Reduce heat slightly and cook until potatoes are just done, but still a little firm.
5. Drain off water.
6. Gently stir in butter OR margarine until melted, being careful not to break apart potatoes.
7. In a small bowl, whisk together milk, flour, salt, and pepper until smooth.
8. Pour milk mixture into potato mixture, stirring gently.
9. Bring to a boil, uncovered. Stir gently and frequently.
10. Reduce heat and simmer, uncovered, for 3 minutes.

Makes 4 servings.

MACARONI SALAD

1 pound salad macaroni, uncooked
boiling water for cooking macaroni
2 tablespoons vegetable oil
1 tablespoon salt
1 cup black olives, chopped
⅓ cup pimientos, chopped
1 cup celery, chopped
1 cup sweet pickle relish
1 ¼ cups mayonnaise or salad dressing
⅓ cup green onions, chopped
1 tablespoon paprika

1. Add oil and salt to boiling water. Cook macaroni until tender.
2. Drain macaroni and place in a large bowl.
3. Add olives, pimientos, celery, sweet pickle relish, mayonnaise or salad dressing, and green onions. Mix together well.
4. Sprinkle paprika evenly over the top.
5. Cover tightly and refrigerate several hours until well-chilled.

Makes 8–10 servings.

DEPRESSION GRAVY

When times were tough, Grandma Opal said she could stretch the budget with this version of the real thing, minus the meat stock.

—J.G.

5 tablespoons flour
2 cups water

⅛ teaspoon pepper
¾ teaspoon salt

1. Heat a heavy skillet over a medium flame.
2. Stir in flour and continue stirring until the flour turns very golden brown.
3. Turn heat to high and whisk in water all at once.
4. Continue whisking until mixture is brought to a full boil.
5. Reduce heat and stir in salt and pepper.
6. Cook 5 minutes, whisking frequently.

Makes about 2 cups.

POTATO SALAD 1

2 pounds potatoes (about 12 small)
5 eggs
½ cup chopped celery
½ cup chopped dill pickle
¼ cup chopped red onion
1 ¼ cups mayonnaise OR salad dressing
1 ½ tablespoons prepared mustard
3 tablespoons pickle juice
1 teaspoon salt

1. Boil potatoes in their skins until tender when pierced with a fork.
2. Allow potatoes to cool. Remove and discard the skins.
3. Cut potatoes into 1-inch chunks.
4. Place eggs in a small saucepan. Add cold water to just cover. Cover and bring to a boil. Remove pan from heat and allow eggs to stand in the water 10 minutes.
5. Remove eggshells and chop eggs into coarse chunks.
6. Gently mix together potatoes, eggs, celery, pickles, onion, mayonnaise, OR salad dressing, mustard, pickle

juice, and salt.

7. Cover and refrigerate for at least 4 hours before serving.

Makes 8 servings.

———————

POTATO SALAD 2

2 pounds potatoes (12 small)
3 eggs
¼ cup chopped green onion tops
⅛ cup diced pimiento
¼ cup chopped celery
½ cup sweet pickle relish
1 ½ cups mayonnaise OR salad dressing
2 tablespoons sugar
½ teaspoon prepared mustard
¾ tablespoon celery seed
¾ teaspoon salt
¼ teaspoon pepper

1. Boil potatoes in their skins until tender when pierced by a fork.
2. Allow potatoes to cool. Remove and discard skins.
3. Cut potatoes into 1-inch chunks.
4. Place eggs in a small saucepan. Add cold water to just cover. Cover and bring to a boil. Remove pan from heat and allow eggs to stand in the water for 10 minutes.
5. In a large mixing bowl, gently combine potatoes, eggs, onion tops, pimiento, celery, and pickle relish.
6. In a medium bowl, whisk together mayonnaise OR salad dressing, sugar, mustard, celery seed, salt, and pepper.
7. Pour dressing over potato mixture and toss gently to coat.
8. Cover and refrigerate at least 4 hours before serving.

Makes 8 servings.

COLESLAW

Grandma Opal grew some of the largest, tastiest vegetables in her garden. She put two together nicely here.

—*J.G.*

4 cups shredded cabbage
½ cup shredded carrots
¼ cup white vinegar
¼ cup sugar
¼ cup mayonnaise
¼ cup milk

1. Place cabbage and carrots into a large bowl that has a tight sealing lid. Set aside.
2. In a small container with a tight sealing lid, add together vinegar, sugar, mayonnaise and milk. Seal and shake well.
3. Pour mixture over cabbage and carrots. Seal bowl and shake well.
4. Refrigerate for at least two hours, inverting bowl occasionally.

Makes 6 servings.

PICKLED BEETS AND EGGS

4 eggs
¾ cup white vinegar
½ cup water
4 tablespoons sugar
¼ teaspoon salt
1 (16 ounce) can sliced beets, reserving juice

1. Boil eggs. Remove and discard shells. Set eggs aside.
2. In a saucepan, combine vinegar, water, sugar, and salt.
3. Bring mixture to a boil and cook until sugar is dissolved.
4. Place eggs in a bowl.
5. Pour beets and reserved juice over eggs.
6. Pour vinegar mixture over beets and eggs.
7. Cover and refrigerate overnight to marinate.

Makes 4 servings.

CARROT SLAW

1 cup raisins
1 ½ cups very hot (not boiling) water
¾ cup mayonnaise
2 tablespoons milk
4 cups grated carrots
¼ teaspoon salt

1. Put raisins in a large bowl and pour hot water over them. Let stand 5 minutes, then drain.
2. In a medium bowl, whisk together mayonnaise and milk until smooth.
3. Stir in raisins, carrots, and salt.
4. Cover and chill at least 1 hour.

Makes 5 servings.

SCALLOPED POTATOES

3 ½ pounds potatoes
2 teaspoons salt, divided
¼ teaspoon pepper, divided

6 tablespoons margarine, divided and cut into small chunks
¾ cup milk
3 tablespoons flour, divided

1. Spray a 13 X 9-inch baking pan with a non-stick cooking spray (This will help tremendously with clean-up.)
2. Peel potatoes and slice into 1/8-inch slices. Divide evenly.
3. In pan, layer ingredients in this order: potatoes, salt, pepper, margarine chunks, flour. Repeat for second layer.
4. Pour milk over top.
5. Cover tightly with foil. Cut several 1-inch slits in foil for ventilation.
6. Bake at 350 degrees for 45 minutes, or until potatoes are tender when pierced by a fork.
7. Remove foil and bake for an additional 20 minutes to brown the top layer of potatoes.

Makes 8 servings.

LIME GELATIN MOLD

Opal was very good for putting together unusual combinations of ingredients to make delicious dishes, like this refreshing salad.

—*J.H.*

1 (6 ounce) box lime-flavored gelatin
2 cups boiling water
1 ¾ cups cold water
16 ounces small curd cottage cheese
1 cup shredded carrots

1. In a large bowl, dissolve gelatin in the boiling water.
2. Stir in cold water.
3. Refrigerate until thickened but still "syrupy."

4. Stir in cottage cheese and carrots.
5. Pour into a 1 ½ quart mold.
6. Refrigerate until firm.
7. Dip bottom of mold into warm water to loosen gelatin.
8. Invert onto a serving plate.

Makes 8 servings.

FRIED GREEN TOMATOES

When Opal first served this tangy dish, I thought she made a mistake. Green tomatoes? Then she told me this was a traditional recipe in the Midwest and South. If you raised tomatoes, you could have a lot ripen at one time. Cooking them when they were green helped use them up before they ripened and had to be canned.

—J.H.

6 green tomatoes
½ cup flour
½ teaspoon salt
¼ teaspoon pepper
6 tablespoons vegetable oil

1. Slice tomatoes into ¼-inch slices.
2. Lay flat on several thicknesses of paper toweling. Press a second layer of paper toweling on top of the tomato slices to squeeze out excess moisture.
3. Allow tomato slices to air-dry on the toweling for an hour to remove even more moisture.
4. In a shallow bowl, mix together flour, salt, and pepper.
5. Heat oil in a heavy skillet over a high flame until very hot.
6. Press tomato slices in flour mixture, coating each side well.
7. Place floured slices in the hot oil, browning each side quickly.
8. Place fried slices on paper toweling to drain off excess oil.

Makes 6 servings.

VEGETABLE DIP

2 cups sour cream
1 tablespoon lemon juice
1 ½ teaspoons minced onion
1 teaspoon celery seed
⅛ teaspoon cayenne pepper
¼ teaspoon garlic salt
½ teaspoon salt
1 ½ teaspoons sugar

1. Mix all ingredients together well.
2. Cover and refrigerate overnight.

Serve with raw vegetables, chips, or crackers.
Makes 2 ¼ cups.

CARROT CAKE

Once again, Grandma's vegetable garden was employed to make this rich, stick-to-your-fork cake.

—J.G.

CAKE:

2 cups sugar
4 eggs
1 ½ cups vegetable oil
3 cups grated carrots
2 cups flour
2 rounded teaspoons baking soda
2 teaspoons cinnamon
1 teaspoon salt

FROSTING:

1 (8 ounce) package cream cheese
16 ounces (1 pound) powdered sugar
½ cup margarine
1 teaspoon vanilla
dash of salt
1 cup chopped walnuts

CAKE:

1. Preheat oven to 350 degrees.
2. Beat together sugar, eggs, and oil until well blended.
3. Stir in carrots.
4. In another bowl, mix together flour, baking soda, cinnamon and salt.
5. Add the flour mixture to the carrot mixture, stirring by hand until just moist.
6. Heavily grease and lightly flour two 9-inch round cake pans.
7. Pour batter evenly into prepared pans.
8. Bake for 45 to 50 minutes, or until the cake leaves the sides of the pan.
9. Let the cake cool in pans for 10 minutes.
10. Invert the pans on wire racks and tap the bottom firmly to loosen the cake enough for it to release from the pan.
11. Cool completely.

FROSTING:

12. Beat together cream cheese, powdered sugar, margarine, vanilla, and salt until smooth.
13. Stir in walnuts
14. Chill for 1 hour.
15. Frost cooled cake.

Store in refrigerator.
Makes 1 2-layer cake.

ORANGE-LEMON CAKE

1 package orange cake mix
5 eggs
1 (3 ounce) box instant lemon pudding mix
½ cup margarine, melted
½ cup milk
½ cup water
1 ½ cups powdered sugar
½ cup lemon juice

1. Preheat oven to 350 degrees.
2. Grease and flour a 9 X 13-inch pan.
3. Mix together cake mix, eggs, pudding mix, margarine, milk, and water until well blended.
4. Pour into prepared pan.
5. Bake for 30–35 minutes, or until a toothpick comes out clean.
6. Remove from the oven.
7. While still hot, use the tines of a large meat fork to poke holes in cake every few inches.
8. To make glaze, combine powdered sugar and lemon juice.
9. Pour glaze over cake, allowing glaze to drizzle down the holes.

Makes one 9 X 13-inch cake.

TANGY LEMON CAKE

Grandma Opal would always warn us about this one: "Get ready to pucker!"

—J.G.

1 package lemon cake mix
1 (1 ounce) box lemon-flavored gelatin
¾ cup water

¾ cup vegetable oil
3 eggs
1 ½ cups powdered sugar
⅓ cup lemon juice
1 teaspoon grated lemon rind

1. Preheat oven to 350 degrees.
2. Grease and flour a 9 X 13-inch pan.
3. In a large mixing bowl, mix together cake mix, gelatin, water, oil, and eggs until well blended.
4. Pour into the prepared pan.
5. Bake for 40 minutes, or until toothpick comes out clean.
6. Allow cake to cool completely in the pan.
7. Using the tines of a large meat fork, poke holes in the cake every few inches.
8. In a small bowl, combine powdered sugar, lemon juice, and lemon rind to make a glaze.
9. Pour glaze evenly over the cake, allowing it to drizzle down the holes.

Makes one 9 X 13-inch cake.

PEAR CAKE

This was another customer favorite at Grandma Opal's diner. The fruit makes it very moist, but not too sweet.

—J.G.

CAKE:

1 (29 ounce) can pears, drained (reserving juice)
1 ½ cups vegetable oil
2 cups sugar
3 eggs
2 cups flour
1 teaspoon salt

1 teaspoon baking soda
1 teaspoon cinnamon
½ cup walnuts or pecans, chopped

VANILLA GLAZE:
¼ cup pear juice (use reserved juice from above)
2 tablespoons margarine, melted
1 ⅔ cups powdered sugar

CAKE:
1. Cut pear slices into coarse chunks. Set aside.
2. In a large mixing bowl, beat together oil, sugar, and eggs until thick and creamy. Set aside.
3. In a smaller bowl, combine flour, salt, baking soda, and cinnamon.
4. Add flour mixture to creamed mixture. Blend together until all ingredients are moistened.
5. Stir in pears and nuts.
6. Grease and flour a 9 X 13-inch pan.
7. Pour evenly into the pan and bake at 350 degrees for 45–50 minutes or until toothpick comes out clean.
8. Remove pan from oven. Allow cake to cool completely. Do not remove the cake from the pan.

VANILLA GLAZE:
1. Mix all ingredients together well.
2. Drizzle over cooled cake.
3. Allow glaze to set before serving.

Makes 1 9 X 13-inch cake.

NUTTY CRACKER PIE

Here's another example of Grandma Opal's ingenuity in using unusual, almost unbelievable ingredients to make delicious creations.

—J.G.

3 egg whites
1 cup sugar
1 teaspoon baking powder
1 teaspoon vanilla
14 saltine crackers, crushed
1 cup walnuts, chopped
whipped cream for topping

1. Grease and flour a 9-inch pie pan.
2. Beat egg whites until soft peaks form. Set aside.
3. In a small bowl, mix together sugar and baking powder.
4. Continue beating egg whites while gradually adding sugar mixture. Beat until stiff peaks form.
5. Fold in vanilla.
6. Add crackers and nuts, stirring well.
7. Spread mixture evenly in the prepared pie pan.
8. Bake at 325 degrees for 30 minutes. (NOTE: The self-forming top crust will crack.)
9. Let cool, then serve with a dollop of whipped cream.

Makes 8 servings.

POTATO CANDY

Opal said this uncommon candy was actually a very common treat during her childhood on her family's farm in West Virginia, as potatoes were plentiful.

—*J.H.*

1 small potato
5 ¼ cups sifted powdered sugar
2–3 drops food coloring
½ teaspoon vanilla
8 tablespoons creamy peanut butter, divided

1. Boil potato in its jacket until tender when pierced with a fork.
2. Drain off water and let potato cool slightly.
3. Remove and discard jacket.
4. Mash potato well.
5. Measure ½ cup of the mashed potato. Discard the rest.
6. Stir in 1 cup of the powdered sugar.
7. Stir in food coloring.
8. Add rest of powdered sugar, blending in well. (NOTE: You may need to mix with your hands to get it thoroughly blended.)
9. Divide the dough and place half on a board dusted with powdered sugar. Cover the remaining half with plastic wrap to keep moist.
10. Dust a rolling pin with powdered sugar and roll dough into a long, rectangular shape, about 12 X 5 inches.
11. Spread half of peanut butter evenly over flattened dough.
12. Loosen dough from board carefully with a spatula.
13. Starting from long edge, roll dough "jelly-roll fashion". pressing together gently but firmly.
14. Repeat steps 10–13 for remaining dough.
15. With a shape knife, cut across rolls to make ½-inch pieces.
16. Lay pieces on waxed paper and allow to dry for at least 4 hours.

Store in a loosely covered container.
Makes about 3 ½ dozen.

COCONUT BALLS

1 cup butter OR margarine, softened
2 pounds powdered sugar
1 (14 ounce) can sweetened condensed milk
4 cups chopped walnuts
15 ounces flaked coconut
30 ounces (2 ½ bags) chocolate chips

3 teaspoons unflavored gelatin
¼ cup boiling water

1. Mix together butter OR margarine, sugar, and milk.
2. Stir in nuts and coconut, mixing well.
3. Cover and chill at least 1 hour.
4. Pull off a small amount and roll into a ball, about 1 inch in diameter.
5. Line a cookie sheet with waxed paper.
6. Place balls in a single layer on cookie sheet.
7. Place sheet into the freezer for 1 hour.
8. Stir gelatin into boiling water. Let stand 5 minutes to dissolve completely.
9. In a double boiler, melt chocolate chips. Whisk in dissolved gelatin until smooth.
10. Remove trays of balls from freezer.
11. Working quickly, roll balls in chocolate, coating completely. (NOTE: Two forks work well for rolling the balls.)
12. Return coated balls to the trays to allow chocolate to set.
13. Store in a covered container in a cool place.

Makes about 10 dozen.

PEANUT BUTTER BALLS

36 ounces creamy peanut butter
1 pound powdered sugar
½ cup butter OR margarine
4 cups crisped rice cereal
18 ounces (1 1/2 bags) chocolate chips
1 (8 ounce) milk chocolate bar
2 teaspoons unflavored gelatin
¼ cup boiling water

1. Combine peanut butter, powdered sugar, butter OR margarine, and cereal.
2. Make into balls, about 1 inch in diameter.
3. Line cookie sheets with a layer of waxed paper.
4. Place balls in a single layer on the sheet.
5. Place sheets in the freezer for 1 hour.
6. Stir gelatin into boiling water. Let stand 5 minutes to dissolve completely.
7. Melt chocolate chips, milk chocolate bar in a double boiler. Whisk in dissolved gelatin until smooth.
8. Remove peanut butter balls from the freezer.
9. Working quickly, roll balls in melted chocolate mixture, coating all sides. (NOTE: Two forks work well to coat the balls.)
10. Return coated balls to trays.
11. Place trays in the refrigerator to allow chocolate to set up.
12. Store peanut butter balls in a covered container in a cool place.

Makes about 7 dozen.

LEMON MERINGUE PIE

Opal's easy tangy pie using fresh lemons will make your mouth water.

—J.H.

¼ cup cornstarch
1 ½ cups water
1 cup sugar
¼ teaspoon salt
3 egg yolks
2 tablespoons margarine
⅓ cup fresh lemon juice
1 ½ tablespoons grated lemon rind
3 egg whites
6 tablespoons sugar
1 9-inch baked pie shell

1. In a small bowl, whisk together cornstarch and water until smooth.
2. In a large saucepan, combine cornstarch mixture, 1 cup sugar, salt, egg yolks, margarine, lemon juice, and lemon rind.
3. Bring mixture to a rolling boil. Cook until thickened, stirring frequently.
4. Remove from heat and allow to cool 15 minutes.
5. To make the meringue, use an electric mixer to beat egg whites together until frothy.
6. Continue beating, slowly adding 6 tablespoons sugar. Keep beating until stiff peaks form.
7. Pour lemon mixture into baked pie shell.
8. Spoon meringue over the lemon mixture, making sure it is completely covered.
9. Bake at 350 degrees for 15-20 minutes, or until top of meringue is lightly browned.
10. Allow to cool before serving.

Makes 1 9-inch pie.

OLD-FASHIONED FUDGE

Grandma Opal told me this was her favorite special treat when she was a little girl because her mother only made it at Christmas time.

1 tablespoon margarine
4 ½ cups sugar
1 can (12 ounce) evaporated milk
18 ounces semi-sweet chocolate chips
1 cup (½ pound) margarine
2 cups chopped nuts (walnuts or pecans)
3 tablespoons vanilla

1. Lightly grease a 15 X 10-inch cookie sheet or jelly roll pan

with the 1 tablespoon of margarine.

2. In a large kettle, add sugar and milk. Stir together well to dissolve sugar.
3. Over medium flame, cook sugar/milk mixture. Stir frequently until it comes to a rolling boil.
4. Reduce heat, but keep at a rolling boil for 6 minutes, stirring frequently.
5. Place remaining ingredients in a large bowl.
6. Pour hot sugar/milk mixture over ingredients and stir together well until everything is melted and dissolved.
7. Pour fudge into greased pan, scraping sides of bowl with a rubber spatula to remove any remaining fudge.
8. Cool for 10 minutes.
9. Place pan of fudge in refrigerator, uncovered for 3 hours, or until firm.
10. Cut into 1-inch squares. Store in air-tight container in refrigerator to keep firm.

Makes approximately 75 squares.

————————

SNOW ON THE MOUNTAIN

In my opinion, this was Grandma Opal's best dessert.
—J.G.

4 eggs
1 cup sugar
1 tablespoon baking powder
½ teaspoon salt
½ cup flour
1 cup chopped dates
1 cup chopped walnuts
1 ½ pints whipping cream
½ cup sugar
½ teaspoon vanilla

1 (16 ounce) can mandarin oranges, drained
1 (20 ounce) can crushed pineapple, drained

1. Preheat oven to 350 degrees.
2. Grease and flour two 8-inch cake pans. Set aside.
3. In a large mixing bowl, beat eggs at high speed. Continue beating as you add 1 cup sugar gradually.
4. In another bowl, combine baking powder, salt, and flour.
5. Fold dry ingredients into egg mixture.
6. Fold in dates and nuts.
7. Pour batter evenly into prepared pans.
8. Bake for 30-35 minutes, or until a toothpick comes out clean.
9. Allow to cool 10 minutes in the pan.
10. Remove cakes from pan and allow to cool completely on a wire rack.
11. Break cake into large pieces.
12. Spread pieces in an ungreased 9 X 13-inch pan.
13. Whip together whipping cream, sugar and vanilla until soft peaks form.
14. Spread half of the whipped cream over cake pieces.
15. Spread oranges and pineapple evenly over whipped cream.
16. Cover fruit with rest of the whipped cream.

Store in the refrigerator.
Makes about 15 servings.

FRESH STRAWBERRY PIE

If you love strawberries, Opal's pie will make you very happy.
—J.H.

1 cup sugar
1 ⅓ cups water
¼ cup cornstarch
¼ cup cold water

2–3 drops red food coloring
1 (3 ounce) box strawberry-flavored gelatin
4–5 small baskets fresh strawberries (about 6–7 cups)
2 8-inch baked pie shells
whipped topping

1. In a saucepan, mix together sugar and 1 ⅓ cups water.
2. Bring to a rolling boil.
3. In a small bowl, whisk together cornstarch and ¼ cup cold water until smooth.
4. Whisk cornstarch mixture into boiling mixture. Continue whisking for 1 minute, making mixture look glossy.
5. Remove from heat. Stir in food coloring.
6. Whisk in gelatin until completely dissolved.
7. Allow mixture to cool at least 30 minutes.
8. Meanwhile, clean and wash strawberries.
9. Let drain in a colander for at least 30 minutes.
10. Place strawberries in a large bowl. Pour sugar mixture over and toss gently to coat thoroughly.
11. Divide strawberries and place in baked pie shells.
12. Divide any leftover liquid and pour evenly over strawberries.
13. Chill at least 1 hour before serving.

Serve with whipped topping.
Makes 2 8-inch pies.

OATMEAL CAKE WITH BROILED TOPPING

1 ½ cups boiling water
1 cup oatmeal
1 cup packed brown sugar
1 cup sugar
½ cup vegetable shortening
2 eggs

1 ⅓ cups cake flour
1 teaspoon baking soda
1 teaspoon cinnamon
½ teaspoon salt
6 tablespoons margarine
1 tablespoon milk
¾ cup packed brown sugar
1 ½ cups flaked coconut
1 cup chopped walnuts OR pecans

1. Preheat oven to 350 degrees.
2. Grease and flour a 9 X 13-inch pan.
3. Place oatmeal in a medium bowl. Pour boiling water over oatmeal and let stand 10 minutes.
4. In a large mixing bowl, cream together 1 cup brown sugar, sugar, and shortening.
5. Beat eggs into creamed mixture.
6. In a medium bowl, mix together cake flour, baking soda, cinnamon, and salt.
7. Blend dry ingredients into creamed mixture.
8. Stir in soaked oats and beat together well.
9. Pour batter into prepared pan.
10. Bake for 30–35 minutes, or until a toothpick comes out clean.
11. Remove from oven and set pan on wire rack. Allow to cool for 10 minutes.
12. To make topping, place margarine, milk, and ¾ cup brown sugar in a saucepan.
13. Bring to a boil and cook 1 minute.
14. Remove from heat and stir in coconut and nuts.
15. Spread topping evenly over warm cake.
16. Place cake under the broiler and broil until topping is lightly browned.
17. Cool completely before serving.

Makes one 9 X 13-inch cake.

DATE CAKE

*A piece of this cake, a cup of hot coffee, and a nice, long
"visit" with Opal are my favorite memories of my mother-in-law.*
                                                         —*J.H.*

1 ½ cups flour
¼ teaspoon baking powder
¼ teaspoon salt
1 cup chopped nuts
1 (8 ounce) package chopped dates
1 teaspoon baking soda
1 cup boiling water
¼ cup butter OR margarine
1 cup sugar
1 egg
1 teaspoon grated lemon peel

1. Preheat oven to 300 degrees.
2. Grease an 8 X 8-inch baking pan.
3. In a medium bowl, mix together flour, baking powder,
   salt, and nuts.
4. In another bowl, mix together dates and baking soda.
5. Pour boiling water over dates and soda. Let stand.
6. Meanwhile, cream together butter OR margarine and sugar.
7. Add egg to creamed ingredients and beat until well mixed.
8. Stir flour mixture into butter mixture.
9. Stir in date mixture (including the water) and lemon peel.
10. Pour batter into the prepared pan.
11. Bake for 1 hour, or until toothpick comes out clean.
12. Cool cake in pan. Cut into squares.

Makes 16 2-inch squares.

DUNKING PLATTERS

2 cups margarine, melted
2 cups packed brown sugar
2 cups sugar
4 eggs
2 teaspoons vanilla
2 cups oatmeal
2 cups wheat flake cereal
4 cups flour
2 teaspoons baking powder
2 teaspoons baking soda

1. In a large mixing bowl, beat together margarine, sugars, eggs, and vanilla for 3 minutes on medium speed.
2. Stir in oats and wheat flake cereal.
3. Blend in flour, baking powder, and baking soda.
4. Place half tablespoons of dough on ungreased cookie sheets.
5. Bake at 350 degrees for about 15 minutes, or until cookies are just starting to turn golden brown.
6. Remove from sheets and cool on a wire rack.

Makes about 6 dozen large cookies.

WEDDING CAKE FROSTING

1 cup vegetable shortening
1 pound (about 4 cups) powdered sugar sifted with 4 tablespoons flour
4 tablespoons milk
2 teaspoons vanilla
1 large egg white

1. Beat together shortening, sifted powdered sugar with flour, milk and vanilla at high speed for 5 minutes.
2. Add egg white and beat for an additional 5 minutes at high speed.

Makes enough to frost one 13 X 9-inch or two round 8-inch cakes.

CHERRY DUMP CAKE

Grandma Opal always kept these ingredients on hand. In case of unexpected company, she said she could literally thrown them together for a fast, moist dessert.

—J.G.

2 cups sugar
2 eggs
½ cup vegetable oil
2 cups flour
2 teaspoons baking soda
1 teaspoon cinnamon
1 teaspoon vanilla
1 cup chopped walnuts
1 (20 ounce) can cherry pie filling
Whipped topping

1. Preheat oven to 350 degrees.
2. Grease and flour a 9 X 13-inch pan.
3. Mix together first eight ingredients until smooth.
4. Blend in cherry pie filling.
5. Pour into prepared pan.
6. Bake for 30–40 minutes, or until toothpick comes out clean.
7. Cool in the pan.
8. Cut into squares and serve with whipped topping.

Makes 1 9 X 13-inch cake.

PINEAPPLE UPSIDE-DOWN CAKE

Opal's rich moist cake has always been a real crowd-pleaser.

—J.H.

2 (20 ounce) cans crushed pineapple, reserving juice
1 ½ cups packed brown sugar
6 tablespoons margarine OR butter
1 package yellow cake mix

1. In a heavy skillet, melt margarine OR butter over a medium flame.
2. Stir in pineapple and reserved juice.
3. Bring mixture to a rolling boil. Reduce heat slightly and continue cooking for 1 hour and 15 minutes to thicken, stirring occasionally.
4. Prepare cake mix according to package instructions.
5. Lightly grease a 9 X 13-inch pan.
6. Spread pineapple mixture evenly into the pan.
7. Spread cake mixture evenly over the top of the pineapple.
8. Bake according to the cake package directions for a 9 X 13-inch pan, testing doneness by inserting a toothpick and seeing if it comes out clean. (NOTE: This cake may take a little longer than time given on the package.)
9. Remove pan from oven and immediately run a knife around the outside of the cake to loosen it from the sides.
10. Quickly turn cake onto a large platter and remove the pan carefully.
11. If any of the pineapple has stuck to the pan, spoon it into its place on the cake.
12. Allow to cool before serving.

Makes 1 9 X 13-inch cake.

ITALIAN DISHES

ITALIAN FAMILY MATRIARCHS
ANNA SEPE
AND
CONNIE SEPE ACUNA

EGGPLANT PARMESAN

When Grandma Anna married her husband, a vegetable peddler, they moved from Italy to America where they continued the vegetable trade. This meant she always had the best vegetables in town for her meals, including eggplants.

—J.H.

1 (1 pound) eggplant
¼ cup flour
6 tablespoons vegetable oil
1 (8 ounce) can tomato sauce
½ teaspoon crushed dried basil
1 egg, beaten
1 tablespoon Parmesan cheese
4 ounces jack OR mozzarella cheese, sliced

1. Preheat oven to 350 degrees.
2. Peel outer skin from eggplant (a potato peeler works well.)
3. Slice eggplant lengthwise into ¼ to ½ inch slices.
4. Place slices in a single layer on paper towels. Place more paper towels over eggplant slices and gently press out excess moisture.
5. Press each slice in flour to coat.
6. Heat oil in a skillet until hot.
7. Quickly brown both sides of the slices.
8. Place fried slices in a colander to drain off excess oil.
9. In a small bowl, mix together tomato sauce and basil.
10. In a 1 ½ quart casserole dish, layer ⅓ of the following ingredients in this order: tomato sauce mixture, eggplant

slices, jack OR mozzarella cheese, Parmesan cheese, and beaten egg. Repeat for two more layers.
11. Cover and bake for 1 hour.
12. Remove from the oven and let stand 15 minutes before serving.

Makes 6 servings.

SPAGHETTI AND MEATBALLS

Grandma Connie was the oldest of eight children and often told me stories of her childhood. She and her family lived a tough but happy life, struggling to make ends meet in the "New Country" during the 1910s and 1920s. This dish was only served on Sundays because it included meat, a luxury. The meals for the rest of the week had a meatless pasta dish as the main course.

—J.G.

½ cup vegetable oil
2–3 pounds 7-bone or round bone roast
2 medium onions, sliced
1 (29 ounce) can tomato puree
2 ½ cups water
1 ½ teaspoons salt
¼ teaspoon pepper
1 tablespoon dried basil
8 ounces French bread
1 cup water
1 ½ pounds hamburger
1 ½ teaspoons salt
¼ teaspoon pepper
¼ cup grated Parmesan cheese
½ teaspoon garlic powder
2 eggs
1 pound spaghetti, uncooked
grated Parmesan cheese

1. Pour ½ cup oil into a large, heavy kettle or pot. Add onions. Place meat on top of onions.
2. Brown onions and meat over low flame for approximately 1 hour. Turn meat and stir onions occasionally. Cook the meat and onions until both are very dark brown.
3. Add tomato puree to meat and onions.
4. Pour 2 ½ cups water into the puree can to loosen any puree left clinging to the can. Add this mixture to the pot. Stir well.
5. Stir in 1 ½ teaspoons salt and ¼ teaspoon pepper.
6. Place basil into the palm of your hand. Rub hands together over the pot, crushing basil into finer pieces. Stir well.
7. Cover and bring sauce to a boil. Reduce heat to the lowest possible flame.
8. Simmer for 2 hours, stirring occasionally.

TO PREPARE MEATBALLS:

9. Place 1 cup water in a small bowl. Dip bread to moisten, squeezing out excess water by hand. Tear bread into 1-inch pieces.
10. In a large bowl, add bread pieces, hamburger, 1 ½ teaspoons salt, ¼ teaspoon pepper, ¼ cup Parmesan cheese, garlic powder, and eggs. Mix well.
11. Form mixture into golf ball-sized meatballs.
12. Heat 3 tablespoons oil in a heavy skillet over a medium flame.
13. Place meatballs into hot skillet. Brown all sides of each meatball well, making sure they are cooked through. Drain on paper towels before adding them to spaghetti sauce.
14. Add cooked meatballs to the sauce.
15. Simmer for 1 hour.
16. Cook spaghetti according to package directions. Drain.
17. Remove roast meat from the sauce before serving sauce. Serve this meat as a side dish, being careful to remove all bones from the sauce, especially those which may have fallen from the meat.
18. Pour sauce over spaghetti. Sprinkle generously with Parmesan cheese.

Makes 6 servings.

SPAGHETTI WITH PEAS

The next four recipes are examples of the meatless pasta dishes served as the main course served Monday through Saturday at my Mom's house when she was growing up.

—J.H.

⅓ cup vegetable oil
½ cup thinly sliced onions
1 (16 ounce) can peas, drained
½ teaspoon salt
⅛ teaspoon pepper
½ pound spaghetti, uncooked

1. Heat oil in skillet over medium heat.
2. Sauté onion until soft and translucent, but not brown.
3. Add peas, salt, and pepper. Simmer for 5 minutes.
4. Cook spaghetti according to package directions. Drain.
5. Place cooked spaghetti in a large, shallow dish or platter.
6. Pour peas/onion mixture over spaghetti.
7. Toss gently to mix.

Makes 4 servings.

SPAGHETTI WITH CAULIFLOWER OR BROCCOLI

1 small head of cauliflower OR 1 small stalk of broccoli
½ pound spaghetti, uncooked
⅓ cup vegetable oil
½ teaspoon garlic powder
¼ teaspoon salt

¼ teaspoon pepper
Parmesan cheese

1. Boil head of cauliflower OR stalk of broccoli until just tender. Remove from water and allow to cool.
2. Cut cauliflower OR broccoli into flowerets. Set aside.
3. Heat oil in a small skillet.
4. Brown garlic powder in hot oil until golden brown. (NOTE: This takes less than a minute!) Remove from heat.
5. Cook spaghetti according to package directions. Drain.
6. Place cooked spaghetti in a large, shallow bowl or platter.
7. Lay cauliflower OR broccoli on top of the spaghetti.
8. Pour garlic/oil mixture over the spaghetti and vegetable and toss well to blend.
9. Sprinkle with Parmesan cheese. Serve immediately.

Makes 3 servings.

PASTA PRIMAVERA

3 medium zucchini squash
4 medium tomatoes
4 cups boiling water
4 cups cold water
1 ½ teaspoons vegetable oil
½ teaspoon garlic powder
1 teaspoon salt
⅛ teaspoon pepper
8 ounces linguini, uncooked
grated Parmesan cheese

1. Slice zucchini into thin slices.
2. Place tomatoes in large bowl. Pour boiling water over tomatoes and let stand 3 minutes.
3. Drain off hot water and add cold water. Let stand for 1 minute.

The skin will now peel off easily.
4. Chop peeled tomatoes into coarse chunks.
5. Heat oil in a large skillet.
6. Add zucchini, tomato, garlic powder, salt, and pepper.
7. Bring to a boil, then reduce heat and simmer until zucchini is tender yet firm.
8. Cook linguini according to package directions.
9. Pour zucchini and tomato mixture over cooked linguini and toss lightly.
10. Sprinkle generously with Parmesan cheese.

Makes 4 servings

———•—•———

LINGUINI WITH OIL AND GARLIC

10 cloves garlic
½ cup vegetable oil
8 ounces linguini, uncooked
grated Parmesan cheese

1. Peel garlic. Slice into thin slices.
2. Pour oil in a saucepan. Add garlic and sauté until golden brown.
3. Prepare linguini according to package directions.
4. Pour oil and garlic mixture over cooked linguini. Toss lightly.
5. Sprinkle generously with cheese.

Makes 4 servings.

———•—•———

CALAMARI (SQUID) AND LINGUINI

When my mom was young, her family lived in San Pedro, a small seaside village in California. At that time, squid was very inexpensive and easy to get. Today it is considered a delicacy. She was a gourmet before her time!

—J.H.

1 pound fresh, uncooked squid
¼ cup vegetable oil
2 cloves garlic, minced
1 tablespoon dried parsley flakes
1 (6-ounce) can tomato paste
2 cups water
1 teaspoon salt
¼ teaspoon pepper
10 ounces linguini, uncooked

1. Clean squid: Cut off pointed end of squid. Grasp the fleshy end with one hand, and the tentacles with the other hand and pull apart. This will remove the internal organs. Make sure everything inside is removed, especially the thin, almost-transparent bone. Wash well, removing the speckled outer skin. Pat dry with paper towels. You will have a fleshy "tube" of meat left after cleaning.
2. Cut across "tube" to make 1-inch rings of squid.
3. In a saucepan, sauté the garlic and parsley in oil until the garlic is golden brown.
4. Add squid rings and cover, stirring frequently. Cook for about 5 minutes, until squid turns a light pink and edges begin to curl.
5. Add water and tomato paste to squid mixture and stir together. Bring to a boil, then reduce heat and simmer uncovered for 30 minutes.
6. Cook linguini until tender but firm and drain.
7. Add squid and sauce to linguini. Toss to combine.

Makes 5 servings.

LINGUINI WITH FISH SAUCE

When times were better, Grandma Anna could substitute a more expensive fish for squid to make this similar dish.

—J.H.

¼ cup plus 2 tablespoons vegetable oil
4 cloves garlic, minced
2 teaspoons dried parsley flakes
1 can (6 ounce) tomato paste
3 cups water
1 ½ teaspoons salt
1 pound fresh fish fillets, boned (such as red snapper or ocean perch)
¾ pound uncooked linguini

1. Heat oil in medium saucepan. Add minced garlic and parsley flakes, stirring occasionally until garlic is golden brown.
2. Add tomato paste, stirring frequently.
3. Add water and salt. Bring to a boil, then reduce heat and continue cooking for 10 minutes.
4. Add fish fillets to sauce and increase heat. Bring to a boil, then cover and reduce heat. Simmer for 40 minutes or until fish is cooked through and flaky.
5. Prepare linguini according to package directions. Drain.
6. Pour fish and sauce over cooked linguini.

Makes 6 servings.

LASAGNA

Grandma Connie said Great-Grandma Anna only served this on special occasions when she was growing up because the sausage and cheese were too expensive.

—J.G.

¼ cup chopped onions
1 tablespoon vegetable oil
¾ pound mild Italian sausage
1 (28 ounce) can tomato puree
1 (16 ounce) can whole tomatoes
1 teaspoon dried basil leaves (crushed)
1 teaspoon salt
1 pound uncooked lasagna noodles
2 cups grated mozzarella cheese, divided
1 pound ricotta cheese, divided
¼ cup grated parmesan cheese, divided

1. Brown onion and sausage in oil until onions are soft.
2. Crush whole tomatoes into smaller pieces.
3. Add tomato pieces, puree and crushed basil leaves to the meat and onion mixture.
4. Bring to a boil, then simmer uncovered for 45 minutes.
5. In a large pot, cook lasagna noodles according to package directions. Divide.
6. In a 9 X 13-inch baking pan, layer ingredients in this order: noodles, sauce, mozzarella cheese, ricotta cheese, and parmesan cheese. Repeat for second layer.
7. Cover tightly with foil.
8. Bake at 350 degrees for 45–60 minutes, or until heated through and cheese is melted.

Makes 12 servings.

ITALIAN MEATLOAF

I always like to make this meatloaf because it reminds me of a giant one of Grandma Anna's meatballs!

—J.H.

1 ½ pounds hamburger
½ pound white bread
1 teaspoon salt
⅛ teaspoon pepper
¼ teaspoon garlic powder
2 eggs
1 (8 ounce) can tomato sauce
2 tablespoons grated parmesan cheese

1. Moisten bread with water, squeezing out excess. Tear bread into small pieces.
2. Mix all ingredients together well.
3. Form into a loaf and place in an ungreased baking pan.
4. Bake uncovered at 350 degrees for 1 hour.

Makes 6-8 servings.

MANICOTTI

¼ cup chopped onion
1 tablespoon vegetable oil
1 (16 ounce) can whole peeled tomatoes
1 (28 ounce) can tomato puree
1 teaspoon crushed basil
1 teaspoon salt
10 manicotti shells uncooked
2 eggs
1 pound grated mozzarella cheese
¼ cup grated Parmesan cheese
2 tablespoons Parmesan cheese
1 pound ricotta cheese

1. In a large skillet, heat oil over a medium flame.
2. Brown onions in the hot oil, stirring frequently.
3. Crush whole tomatoes into coarse pieces.

4. Add the coarse tomato pieces, tomato puree, basil, and salt to the browned onions. Stir together.
5. Cover and bring to a boil.
6. Reduce heat and simmer for 45 minutes.
7. Cook manicotti shells according to package directions.
8. Drain and rinse shells under cool water.
9. In a medium bowl, mix together eggs, mozzarella cheese, ¼ cup Parmesan cheese, and ricotta cheese.
10. Stuff about ½ cup of the cheese mixture into each manicotti shell. (NOTE: You can carefully spoon this in, or use a pastry bag or food gun.)
11. Spread ¼ cup of prepared sauce on the bottom of a 9 X 13-inch baking pan.
12. Place stuffed shells in the pan, making two layers if necessary.
13. Pour remaining sauce over shells.
14. Sprinkle 2 tablespoons Parmesan cheese evenly over the shells.
15. Cover with foil and bake at 375 degrees for 1 hour.

Makes 5 servings.

BREADED BEEF CUTLETS

Believe it or not, Grandma Anna served these as a sidedish at family get-togethers, along with appetizers, eggplant parmesan, and several pasta dishes. Today we serve it as a main dish.
—J.H.

1 pound beef cube steaks
½ teaspoon salt
¼ teaspoon pepper
1 egg
6 tablespoons vegetable oil, separated
32 saltine cracker squares

1. Crush crackers into fine crumbs, set aside on a sheet of waxed paper.
2. In a shallow bowl, beat together egg, salt and pepper.
3. Dip meat into egg mixture to coat.
4. With palm of hand, firmly press meat into cracker crumbs until well breaded. This will flatten and enlarge the piece of meat.
5. In a heavy skillet, heat 3 tablespoons vegetable oil over a medium-high flame.
6. Brown breaded meat in the oil, making sure it is cooked through. Add more oil as needed when frying.
7. Remove from pan and drain off excess oil on paper towels.

Makes 4 servings.

BEAN & TOMATO ON BREAD

Mom said when money was scarce (as it often was), this simple dish would see them through.

—J.H.

2 cups small dried white beans
2 (16 ounce) cans whole peeled tomatoes
4 cups water
1 teaspoon salt
½ teaspoon pepper
3 teaspoons dried minced onion
1 pound loaf French bread, uncut

1. Clean and wash beans.
2. Put beans, tomatoes, water, salt, pepper and dried onion in a large kettle.
3. Bring to a boil, then cover and reduce heat.
4. Simmer for 3 hours, or until beans are tender but still juicy.
5. Cut thick slices of the French bread.
6. Pour beans and juice over bread.

Makes 5 servings.

STUFFED BEEF TONGUE IN SAUCE

1 beef tongue (about 4 or 5 pounds)
3 small eggs
2 tablespoons vegetable oil
¼ teaspoon garlic powder
2 (8 ounce) cans tomato sauce
1 cup water
½ teaspoon Italian seasoning
½ teaspoon salt
⅛ teaspoon pepper

1. Place tongue in a large kettle and just cover with water.
2. Cover and bring to a boil.
3. Reduce heat just enough to keep water boiling. Cook for 2 hours, or until meat is very tender when pierced with a fork.
4. Remove meat from water and allow it to cool 15 minutes.
5. Boil eggs. Discard the shells and set aside.
6. Cut off 2–3 inches of the tip of the tongue as well as the back connecting meat, leaving about 6 inches of center cut. (NOTE: The excess meat can be sliced to make a very lean lunch meat.)
7. Trim away the thick, whitish layer of skin from the center cut and discard.
8. Using a carving knife with a 1-inch blade, carefully cut a tunnel through the length of the piece of meat.
9. Gently press boiled eggs into the tunnel. (NOTE: If it is too tight a fit, cut a bigger tunnel.)
10. In a large saucepan, heat oil over a medium flame.
11. Add garlic powder and sauté until golden brown.
12. Stir in tomato sauce, water, Italian seasonings, salt, and pepper.
13. Bring to a boil.
14. Place stuffed tongue in pan, basting sauce over the top.

15. Cover and reduce heat.
16. Simmer for 1 hour, basting occasionally.
17. Slice into ½-inch slices.

Makes 5 servings.

———— • • ————

ZUCCHINI FRITTATA

1 ½ tablespoons vegetable oil
¼ teaspoon garlic powder
3 medium zucchini, sliced
1 large tomato, peeled and chopped
6 eggs
2 tablespoons grated Parmesan cheese
1 cup grated cheddar cheese
½ teaspoon salt
⅛ teaspoon pepper

1. Heat oil in a skillet over a medium flame.
2. Add garlic powder and zucchini slices and sauté until zucchini is a golden brown.
3. Stir in tomato and heat through.
4. In a bowl, beat eggs together slightly.
5. Add cheeses, salt, and pepper to eggs. Stir together.
6. Pour egg mixture into the skillet. Allow egg to cook on one side.
7. Carefully flip frittata over. Allow other side to cook, checking to make sure the middle is also getting cooked through.

Serve immediately.
Makes 4 servings.

———— • • ————

POACHED EGGS IN SAUCE

2 cups prepared spaghetti sauce
4 eggs
salt and pepper to taste

1. In a skillet, heat sauce to a boil.
2. Carefully break eggs into sauce, trying not to break the yolks.
3. Reduce heat and simmer 5 minutes, occasionally spooning sauce over eggs until cooked.
4. Serve, adding salt and pepper.

Makes 2 servings.

PIZZA

These individual pizzas with a light, airy crust were always a favorite around Grandma Anna's house.

—J.H.

2 cups flour
1 ¼ cups warm (120 degree) water
¼ cup vegetable oil
1 package (1/4 ounce) active dry yeast
1 ½ cups flour
extra flour for kneading
1 teaspoon vegetable oil
1 cup vegetable oil (for frying)
2 ½–3 cups prepared spaghetti sauce
3–3 ½ cups grated cheddar cheese
Pizza toppings as desired (grated Parmesan cheese, pepperoni, ham, mushrooms olives, onion, etc.)

1. In a large mixing bowl, combine flour, water, ¼ cup vegetable oil, and yeast. Mix together for 3 minutes on

medium speed.

2. Stir in 1 ½ cups flour and mix by hand until the dough forms a soft ball.
3. Knead dough on a lightly floured board for 5 minutes, adding more flour if it starts to stick.
4. Coat the sides of a large bowl with 1 teaspoon oil.
5. Place the dough in the bowl, turning it over once or twice to make sure all sides are oiled.
6. Cover the bowl and allow it to rise in a warm place until doubled.
7. Punch the dough down and cover again. Allow the dough to rise in a warm place until it has doubled again.
8. In a heavy skillet, heat 1 cup oil over a medium flame.
9. On a lightly floured board, roll out about ½ cup of dough until it is about ⅛-inch thick and about 7 inches in diameter.
10. Quickly fry dough in hot oil, lightly browning each side of crust.
11. Drain crusts on paper toweling to remove excess oil.
12. Spread about ¼ cup spaghetti sauce evenly over each crust.
13. Sprinkle about ⅓ cup grated cheese on each.
14. Top with desired pizza toppings.
15. Place pizzas on cookie sheets and bake in a 375 degree oven for 5 minutes, or until cheese is melted and bubbly.

Serve hot.
Makes 8–10 individual pizzas.

RIBS AND CABBAGE STEW

3 pounds country-style pork ribs
1 tablespoon vegetable oil
½ teaspoon garlic powder
6 cups water
1 teaspoon salt
⅛ teaspoon pepper
1 medium head of cabbage
4 medium potatoes

1. In a large pot, heat oil over a medium flame.
2. Sauté garlic powder in hot oil until golden brown.
3. Place ribs in pot and quickly brown all sides.
4. Add water, salt, and pepper.
5. Cover and bring to a boil.
6. Reduce heat and simmer for 2 hours, or until meat is very tender.
7. Cut cabbage head into eighths.
8. Peel potatoes and cut into 1-inch cubes.
9. Add cabbage and potatoes to the pot.
10. Cover and bring to a boil.
11. Reduce heat and simmer for 30 minutes or until potatoes and cabbage are tender but firm.

Makes 4 servings.

CHEESE STUFFED PEPPERS

2 large bell peppers
2 cups moist French bread pieces
½ cup grated cheddar cheese
1 egg
⅛ teaspoon salt
pinch of pepper
⅛ teaspoon garlic powder
½ cup water

1. To clean bell pepper, cut off tops and remove seeds, rinsing well.
2. Mix together remaining ingredients well.
3. Divide mixture and put into peppers.
4. Place peppers in a 1-quart casserole dish.
5. Pour water into bottom of dish.
6. Cover and bake at 350 degrees for 1 ¼ hours, or until peppers are tender when pierced with a fork.

Makes 2 servings.

ITALIAN VEGETABLE SOUP

This is another low-cost meal that Great-Grandma Anna used to stretch her food budget.

—*J.G.*

1 beef shin OR meaty soup bone
3 quarts (12 cups) water
1 ½ cups sliced carrots
1 ½ cups sliced celery
1 cup sliced onion
1 (8 ounce) can tomato sauce
2 teaspoons salt
¼ teaspoon pepper
¾ cup rice, uncooked
grated Parmesan cheese

1. In a large kettle, combine beef, water, carrots, celery, onion, tomato sauce, salt, and pepper.
2. Cover and bring to a boil.
3. Reduce heat and simmer 1 ½ hours, or until meat is very tender.
4. Remove meat from bone. Return meat pieces to the kettle. Discard bone.
5. Add rice to ingredients in the kettle.
6. Cover and return to a boil.
7. Reduce heat and simmer for 30 minutes.

Serve hot with plenty of cheese sprinkled on the top.
Makes 6-8 servings.

"WE MUST BE CHINESE SOMEWHERE DOWN THE FAMILY TREE" CHICKEN AND RICE

Where this recipe came from, no one can remember. But it was always a family favorite!

—J.H.

5 pieces of chicken (leg, thigh, or breast)
¼ teaspoon garlic powder
4 cups water
1 tablespoon oil
½ cup thinly sliced onion
½ cup thinly sliced bell pepper
1 tablespoon soy sauce
2 chicken bouillon cubes
½ teaspoon salt
¼ cup cornstarch
¼ cup cold water
1 cup rice, uncooked
tomato wedges for garnish

1. Place chicken in a large pot. Add 4 cups water and garlic powder.
2. Cover and boil until chicken is tender.
3. Remove chicken, saving 3 cups of the broth.
4. Discard skin and bone. Cut chicken into coarse chunks.
5. In a skillet, sauté onions in oil until soft.
6. Add chicken broth, bell peppers, bouillon cubes, and soy sauce.
7. Cover and bring to a boil.
8. In a small bowl, mix together cornstarch and ¼ cup water. Whisk into boiling ingredients.
9. Cook for 5 minutes, stirring occasionally.
10. Add chicken pieces. Cook for 3 minutes.
11. Cook rice according to package directions.

Serve chicken mixture over rice. Garnish with tomato wedges. Makes 4 servings.

CHOW MEIN

Here's another recipe that has no connection to our family history, but was one of Grandma Connie's favorites.

—*J.G.*

2 cups diced chicken breast OR pork steak
2 tablespoons flour
2 tablespoons vegetable oil
½ teaspoon garlic powder
1 cup sliced onion
1 cup water
1 ½ cups sliced celery
1 bell pepper, sliced
3 cups bean sprouts
2 cups sliced mushrooms
3 tablespoons soy sauce

1. Dredge chicken OR pork in flour to coat.
2. Heat oil in large skillet over a high flame.
3. Add coated meat and garlic to hot oil, stirring until meat is just cooked through.
4. Add onion. Continue cooking until onion is soft and translucent.
5. Stir in water, celery, and bell pepper.
6. Cover and bring to a boil.
7. Reduce heat and simmer for 15 minutes, or until celery and bell pepper are tender but firm.
8. Stir in bean sprouts, mushrooms, and soy sauce.
9. Cover and continue cooking for 5–10 minutes.

Serve with steamed white rice.
Makes 6 servings.

SPAGHETTI FRITTATA

In the rare case of any leftover spaghetti after her family of ten had their fill, Grandma Anna would make this simple yet hearty dish.

—J.H.

4 cups cold, cooked spaghetti
3 eggs, slightly beaten
½ teaspoon salt
⅛ teaspoon pepper
¼ teaspoon garlic powder
⅓ cup grated Parmesan cheese
3 tablespoons vegetable oil

1. In a large bowl, mix together spaghetti, eggs, salt, pepper, garlic powder, and cheese.
2. Heat oil in a skillet over a high flame.
3. Place spaghetti mixture in the hot oil, spreading it out to fit the pan.
4. Cook until bottom is well browned.
5. Flip spaghetti mixture over and cook other side until browned.

Serve immediately.
Makes 5 servings.

PICKLED ZUCCHINI

3 large zucchini squash (about 9 inches long)
½ cup vegetable oil for frying (more if needed)
2 tablespoons wine vinegar
⅛ garlic powder
¼ teaspoon salt
¼ teaspoon crushed red peppers

1. Slice zucchini into thin slices.
2. Spread slices on paper towels in a single layer to dry for 1 hour.
3. Heat oil in a large frying pan.
4. Sauté zucchini, one layer at a time, until dark golden brown. Place in a colander to drain.
5. Place zucchini in a bowl that has a tight-fitting lid.
6. Add vinegar, garlic powder, salt, and crushed peppers. Toss well.
7. Cover and refrigerate for at least 3 hours for flavors to blend. (NOTE: Overnight is better.)

Makes 4 servings.

FRIED SQUASH BLOSSOMS

Mom told me that very little food was ever wasted, as this recipe shows.

—J.H.

8–10 squash blossoms (picked from a growing zucchini or summer squash plant)
1 cup flour
1 egg
½ + ⅛ cup milk
2 tablespoons vegetable oil

1. Pick blossoms in the morning when they are open.
2. Remove center parts and stem of the blossom.
3. Wash well and lay out on paper toweling to dry. (NOTE: Blossoms must be completely dry!)
4. Make a batter by mixing together flour, egg, and milk in a shallow bowl.
5. Heat oil in a skillet over a high flame.
6. Dip dry blossoms in the batter.
7. Place battered blossoms in the hot oil, frying both sides quickly.
8. Remove and drain on paper toweling to remove excess oil.

Makes 2–3 servings.

POTATO FRITTATA

While pasta was the main source of carbohydrates, the potato didn't escape Great-Grandma Anna's Italian touch!
—*J.G.*

5 medium potatoes
1 cup grated cheddar cheese
2 tablespoons grated Parmesan cheese
3 eggs
¼ cup sliced green onions
¾ teaspoon salt
⅛ teaspoon pepper
⅛ teaspoon garlic powder
1 teaspoon vegetable oil

1. Peel potatoes and cut into coarse chunks.
2. Boil until just tender.
3. Drain off water and mash potatoes. (Do not add any liquid or butter.)
4. Mix in cheeses, onions, eggs, salt, pepper, and garlic powder.
5. Spread oil evenly in a 9-inch pie pan.
6. Pat potato mixture firmly into the pan.
7. Bake at 375 degrees for 40 minutes, or until top is golden brown.
8. Remove from oven and let stand for 5 minutes before serving.

Makes 6 servings.

ITALIAN SALAD DRESSING

Grandma Connie used this basic recipe for marinating vegetables, dressing on submarine sandwiches, and, of course, for tossing into green salads.

—J.G

¼ cup wine vinegar
2 tablespoons water
¾ cup vegetable or olive oil
½ teaspoon garlic powder
¾ teaspoon salt
⅛ teaspoon pepper

1. Shake all ingredients together in a cruet with a stopper top, or in a tightly-covered container.
2. Pour over salads, vegetables, or on bread for submarine sandwiches. (NOTE: Store tightly covered in the refrigerator. Shake well before using.)

Makes about 1 cup.

———————

EGGPLANT PATTIES

1 eggplant (about 1 pound)
2 eggs
1 tablespoon Parmesan cheese
¼ teaspoon salt
⅛ teaspoon pepper
⅛ teaspoon garlic powder
3 ¼ cups dry bread pieces, about 1 X 1"
2 tablespoons vegetable oil

1. Peel eggplant and cut into eighths.
2. Steam eggplant pieces until tender. Let cool.

3. In a large bowl, combine cooled eggplant, eggs, cheese, salt, pepper, garlic powder, and bread crumbs. Mix together well. (NOTE: mixture will be very soft.)
4. Heat oil in a skillet over a medium flame.
5. Form eggplant mixture into small patties.
6. Place patties in the hot oil, browning each side.
7. Drain patties on paper towels to remove excess oil.

Makes 8-10 patties.

FRIED CAULIFLOWER

The following three recipes were always served by Grandma Anna as appetizers at family dinners.

—J.H.

1 large head cauliflower
½ cup flour
3 eggs
¾ teaspoon salt, divided
⅛ teaspoon pepper, divided
½ vegetable oil

1. Peel outer leaves from head of cauliflower. Trim stem, but keep head intact.
2. Place head, stem down, in a large saucepan. Add about 1 inch of water.
3. Cover and bring to a boil.
4. Reduce heat and steam for 15 minutes, or until cauliflower is firm but tender.
5. Remove cauliflower and allow to cool enough to handle, about ten minutes.
6. Cut into flowerets and allow to cool completely.
7. In a shallow bowl, combine flour and half of salt and pepper.
8. In another bowl, beat together egg and rest of salt and pepper.

9. Heat oil in a skillet over a high flame.
10. Dip flowerets first in the flour mixture, then in egg mixture.
11. Place coated flowerets in the hot oil, quickly browning all sides until golden.
12. Remove and drain on paper toweling to remove excess oil.

Makes approximately 18 flowerets.

FRIED CELERY

7 or 8 ribs celery
½ cup flour
2 eggs
¾ teaspoon salt, divided
⅛ teaspoon pepper, divided
½ cup vegetable oil

1. Peel outer layer of celery to remove any tough strands.
2. Cut ribs into 4-inch lengths.
3. Steam celery until tender but firm.
4. In a shallow bowl, combine flour, half of salt, and half of pepper.
5. In another shallow bowl, beat together eggs with the rest of the salt and pepper.
6. Heat oil in a skillet over a high flame.
7. Dip celery ribs first in flour mixture, then egg mixture.
8. Place ribs in hot oil and quickly brown both sides until golden brown.
9. Remove and place on paper toweling to remove excess oil.

Makes approximately 18 ribs.

FRIED ARTICHOKE HEARTS

3 large artichokes
½ cup flour
3 eggs
¾ teaspoon salt, divided
⅛ teaspoon pepper, divided
½ cup vegetable oil

1. Trim off stem and snap off outer leaves until you get to the heart. Cut off row of thorns at the top of the heart.
2. Cut hearts into fourths.
3. Place pieces in a large saucepan. Add about 1 inch of water.
4. Cover and bring to a boil.
5. Reduce heat and steam for 15 minutes, or until hearts are firm but tender.
6. Remove hearts and allow to cool enough to handle, about 10 minutes.
7. In a shallow bowl, combine flour and half of salt and pepper.
8. In another shallow bowl, beat together egg and rest of salt and pepper.
9. Heat oil in a skillet over a high flame.
10. Dip hearts first in the flour mixture, then in egg mixture.
11. Place coated hearts in the hot oil, quickly browning all sides until golden.
12. Remove and drain on paper toweling to remove excess oil.

Makes 12 pieces.

GREEN BEAN AND POTATO SALAD

1 ¼ pounds fresh green beans
2 pound potatoes
1 ½ cups sliced red onion
¼ cup wine vinegar

2 tablespoons water
¾ cup vegetable oil
½ teaspoon garlic powder
¾ teaspoon salt
⅛ teaspoon pepper

1. Cut off ends of green beans and break into 1-inch pieces. Rinse well.
2. Place beans in a 3 quart saucepan and add water to cover.
3. Cover and bring to a boil. Reduce heat.
4. Simmer beans for 15 to 20 minutes, or until tender.
5. Drain off water and rinse beans under cool running water to stop cooking process and cool the beans.
6. Boil unpeeled potatoes until tender when pierced by a fork. Cool until easy to handle.
7. Peel and slice potatoes into ¼-inch slices.
8. In a large bowl, place beans, potatoes, onion slices, vinegar, water, oil, garlic powder, salt, and pepper. Toss gently to mix.
9. Cover well and refrigerate for at least 4 hours, stirring occasionally.

Makes 8 servings.

ROASTED PEPPER SALAD

I remember watching with fascination as Grandma Connie made this salad. She would turn the peppers by hand, which always amazed me how she never burned herself. Also, the roasted peppers had a distinctive, wonderful aroma. Now when I make this, I think of Grandma and smile.

—J.G.

4 bell peppers (green or red)
cold water
4 cloves garlic, sliced

⅛ teaspoon pepper
½ teaspoon salt
2 tablespoons oil

1. Place whole bell pepper directly on the flame or burner of the stove. Toast all sides until well blackened.
2. Place toasted peppers in a large bowl. Cover with cold water until cooled.
3. Rub off the toasted skin of the bell pepper with your hands. Discard skin.
4. Cut bell peppers in half and remove seeds and fibrous parts of the middle.
5. Cut peppers into 1-inch strips and place in a bowl.
6. Add garlic, pepper, salt, and oil to peppers and toss well to mix.
7. Cover well and refrigerate for at least 3 hours before serving.

Serve cold.
Makes 6 servings.

BREAD PATTIES

Grandma Connie used this recipe whenever she had too much bread in the house. It's great served with a grilled steak and salad.

—J.G.

7 cups day-old bread pieces (about 1/2-inch pieces)
warm water
2 eggs
¼ cup grated Parmesan cheese
¼ teaspoon salt
⅛ teaspoon pepper
¼ teaspoon garlic powder, divided
1 (8 ounce) can tomato sauce
1 cup water
vegetable oil for frying (as needed)

1. Moisten bread pieces with warm water until it just sticks together in a ball.
2. Mix in eggs, cheese, salt, pepper, and garlic powder.
3. Using ⅓ cup of the mixture at a time, form into patties.
4. Heat oil in a skillet over a medium flame.
5. Place patties in hot oil and brown each side until a dark golden color.
6. Remove patties and place on paper toweling to drain off excess oil. Do not discard oil.
7. Stir tomato sauce and water into remaining oil in the skillet.
8. Return patties to the skillet, spooning sauce over the patties.
9. Cover and bring to a boil.
10. Reduce heat and simmer for 20 minutes, flipping patties over occasionally.

Makes 6 servings.

GARLIC TOAST

1 (1 pound) loaf French bread, unsliced
½ cup (1 stick) butter OR margarine
1 teaspoon garlic powder

1. Cutting on a diagonal, slice the bread into 1-inch pieces. Set aside.
2. Melt butter OR margarine in a shallow pan or bowl.
3. Stir in garlic powder.
4. Dip one side of the bread slice into the butter-garlic mixture.
5. Broil bread, buttered side up, until golden brown. (NOTE: Watch it closely because it can burn quickly.)

Makes 12-15 slices.

RED GREEN BEANS

1 tablespoon vegetable oil
¼ teaspoon garlic powder
1 (8 ounce) can tomato sauce
¼ cup water
⅛ teaspoon pepper
1 (16 ounce) can green beans, drained

1. In a saucepan, heat oil over a medium flame.
2. Brown garlic until golden brown.
3. Add tomato sauce, water and pepper.
4. Bring to a boil, then reduce heat.
5. Simmer 2 to 3 minutes.
6. Stir in green beans.
7. Cover and bring to a boil.
8. Reduce heat and simmer 5 minutes.

Makes 4 servings.

ITALIAN COOKIES

Grandma Anna's cookies are my favorites. They make great "dunkers" in coffee or milk. I think of her every time I make them.

—J.H.

FROSTING:
1 cup sifted powdered sugar
2 tablespoons milk
2–3 drops food coloring

COOKIE:
4 eggs
1 cup vegetable oil

1 ½ cups sugar
4 teaspoons baking powder
1 ½ teaspoons vanilla
¼ teaspoon salt
1 (5 ounce) can evaporated milk
6 ½ cups flour*

1. In a small bowl, mix together powdered sugar, milk, and food coloring. Set aside.
2. Preheat oven to 350 degrees.
3. Using the medium speed of a mixer, blend together eggs, oil, sugar, baking powder, vanilla, salt, and milk for 3 minutes.
4. Gradually sift in flour while stirring by hand. (*NOTE: dough should be soft enough to roll without sticking to your hand. Extra flour may be needed to reach this consistency.)
5. Pull off "ping-pong ball" sized amounts of dough.
6. Roll between hands to form a 3 inch long "rope" of dough.
7. Bend into the shape of a crescent and place on ungreased cookie sheet.
8. Bake for 10-12 minutes, or until you can touch it lightly and no fingerprint is left. (NOTE: The bottom will be lightly browned but the top will still be white when done.)
9. Remove cookies immediately from sheet.
10. Dip top of hot cookie into powder sugar mixture.
11. Place on wire rack to cool.

Makes 6-7 dozen cookies.

FRIED BUBBLES IN HONEY

One of my earliest recollections of my Grandma Anna involves this unusual dessert. She made it every Christmas Eve for any family members or friends who dropped by. Now when I make it during the holidays, the taste really brings back wonderful childhood memories.

—J.H.

DOUGH:

- 2 cups flour
- ¼ cup sugar
- 3 eggs, slightly beaten
- ¼ cup vegetable oil
- 1 teaspoon grated lemon rind
- extra flour (as needed)
- 1 cup vegetable oil (for frying)

COATING:

- ½ cup honey
- ½ tablespoon sugar
- ½ cup candied lemon peel
- Nonpareil candies (for decorating)

DOUGH:

1. In a large mixing bowl, combine sugar and flour.
2. In another bowl, combine eggs, 1/4 cup vegetable oil, and lemon rind.
3. Stir egg mixture into flour mixture. (NOTE: The dough will be very soft.)
4. Turn dough onto a lightly floured board. Kneed for 3 minutes so that dough becomes smooth and stretchy. Add a little more flour if it starts to stick to the board.
5. Flatten dough into a circle about 6 inches across and ¾-inch thick.
6. Cut long strips of dough, about ½-inch wide.
7. With lightly-floured hands, roll strips between your palms to make ropes, about ½-inch thick.
8. Cut ropes into ½-inch pieces.
9. In a heavy skillet, heat 1 cup oil over a medium-high flame.
10. Add enough dough pieces to make a single layer in the hot oil. Brown all sides, stirring frequently.
11. Remove and place on paper toweling to drain off excess oil.
12. Repeat steps 10 and 11 until all dough is cooked.

COATING:

13. In a small saucepan, heat honey and sugar until sugar is

just dissolved and mixture is almost to a boil.
14. Stir in candied lemon peel. Remove pan from heat.
15. Place fried bubbles in a shallow bowl.
16. Pour honey coating over the bubbles and toss gently. Allow to cool for 5 minutes.
17. Arrange fried bubbles in honey in a mound on a serving platter.
18. Sprinkle with nonpareil candies to decorate.

Serve warm.
Makes 8–10 servings.

ALMOND COOKIES

2 cups sugar
¾ cup vegetable shortening
7 eggs
1 teaspoon vanilla
3 cups flour
3 rounded teaspoons baking powder
3 ¾ cups shelled and halved almonds

1. In a large mixing bowl, cream sugar and shortening until fluffy.
2. Add eggs to the sugar/shortening mixture and beat together until light and creamy.
3. Add vanilla to the mixture and continue beating briefly to blend in vanilla.
4. In a medium bowl, mix together flour and baking powder.
5. Slowly and thoroughly blend flour mixture into sugar mixture.
6. Stir in almond pieces.
7. Cover bowl with plastic wrap or foil. Refrigerate for at least 4 hours. (NOTE: Overnight is fine.)
8. Preheat oven to 375 degrees.
9. Drop by rounded teaspoon on an ungreased baking sheet.

10. Bake for 10 minutes.
11. Remove sheet from oven and allow cookies to stand on the sheet for 1 minute.
12. Remove cookies and cool on wire rack.

Makes about 9 dozen cookies.